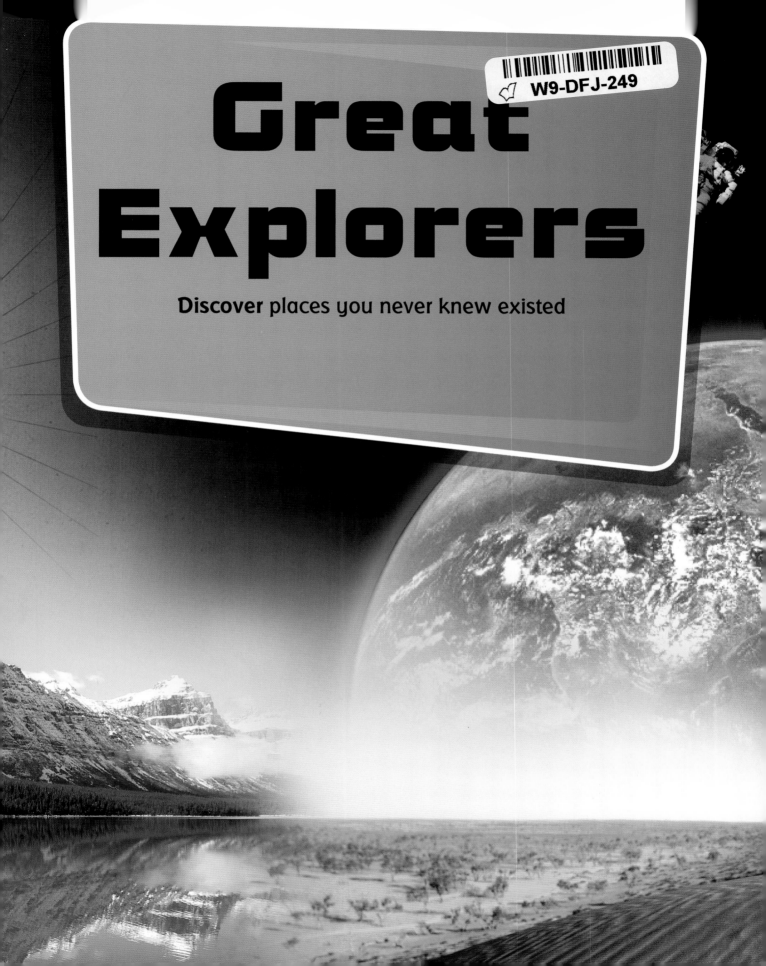

Great Explorers

Discover places you never knew existed

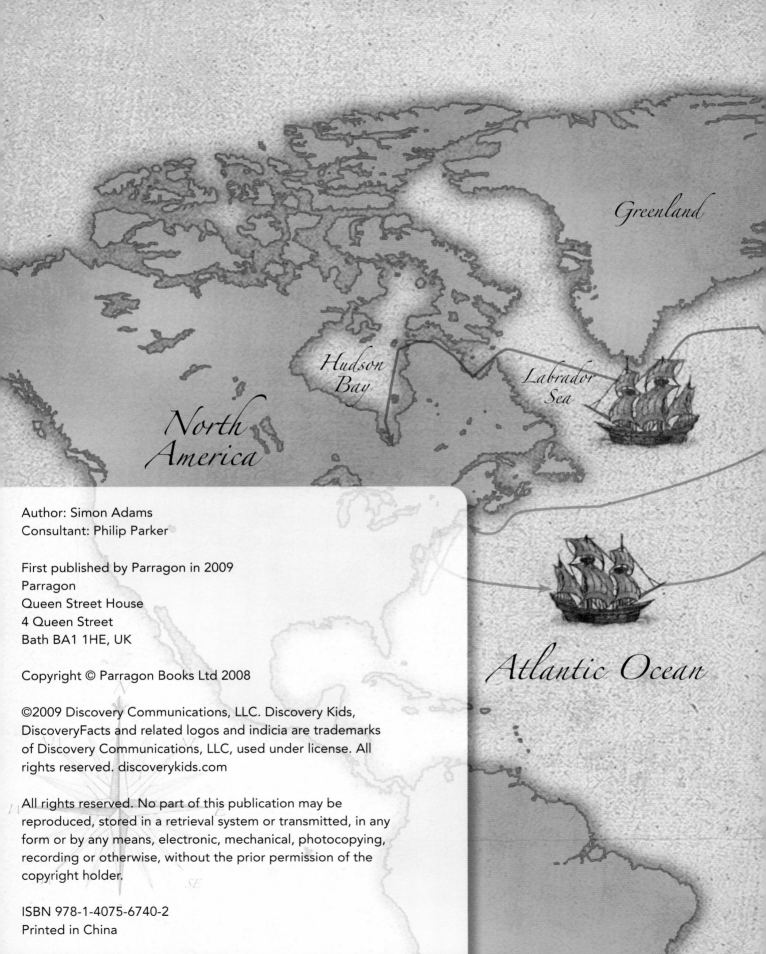

Greenland

North
America

Hudson
Bay

Labrador
Sea

Atlantic Ocean

Author: Simon Adams
Consultant: Philip Parker

First published by Parragon in 2009
Parragon
Queen Street House
4 Queen Street
Bath BA1 1HE, UK

ISBN 978-1-4075-6740-2
Printed in China

Contents

Introduction

Human beings once lived only in East Africa. People first left this region about 50,000 years ago, and ever since we have been driven by the urge to explore. Brave explorers have pushed back the frontiers and reached the most hostile places on Earth. Every continent has been explored, from the tropical jungles to the icy poles, and many have lost their lives in the process. Recently, we have even begun to discover what lies beyond our planet. Here we tell the stories of some extraordinary explorers, from the first journeys ever recorded to modern-day adventurers. These are the explorations that have shaped the world we know today.

Early Explorers

The first travelers all set out on their journeys for a reason. The Egyptians and Phoenicians traveled for trade. The Chinese left home to find new allies. The Norsemen set sail in search of new places to live. Muslims made the hajj or pilgrimage to Mecca. We know about these early adventurers because some of them wrote about their journeys, which took them to the very edges of their known world.

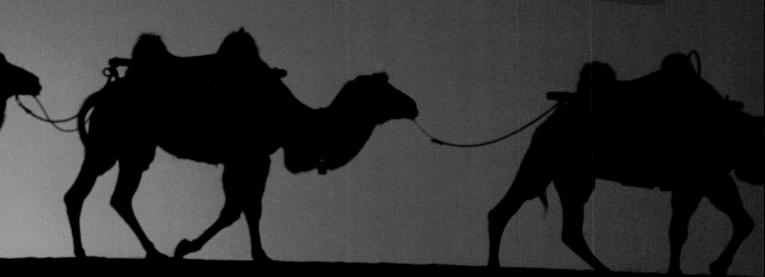

Punt voyage

We do not know the name of the first explorer. However, we do know that the ancient Egyptians undertook a voyage to a place called Punt about 3,500 years ago, during the reign of Queen Hatshepsut.

Queen Hatshepsut

Hatshepsut ruled Egypt around 1473–1458 B.C. She was often portrayed in statues as a man. This is because it was almost unheard of at the time for a woman to become a pharaoh (Egyptian ruler).

By land and sea

After making contact with the people of Punt, the Egyptians traveled there in order to trade. We do not know where Punt was, but it may have been in northern Somalia, at the end of the Red Sea. The Egyptians dragged all the materials they needed to build their ships overland from the Nile River to the Red Sea coast. There they built five ships and sailed south for a year.

Hatshepsut's temple

Hatshepsut built a huge temple in which to protect her body when she died. The temple is built into cliffs on the west bank of the Nile River at Thebes, one of the main religious centers of Egypt.

Carvings on the temple walls tell us about the voyage to Punt.

The riches of Punt

Once in Punt, the Egyptians loaded their ships with myrrh trees, incense, ivory, ebony, gold, leopard skins, and other luxuries. They also took live animals with them, such as baboons and pet dogs. Once their ships were full, they sailed north again up the Red Sea. They crossed over land once more to the Nile River and sailed home.

Hatshepsut's temple walls depict the triumphant return of the sailors from Punt.

Time Line

c.**2500 B.C.**
Ancient Egyptians first make contact with Punt

c.**1473 B.C.**
Hatshepsut rules on behalf of her infant stepson Thutmose III

c.**1470 B.C.**
Hatshepsut orders the voyage to Punt to bring back precious items for her temples and palaces

c.**1458 B.C.**
Hatshepsut dies

DiscoveryFact™

Queen Hatshepsut erected four obelisks in the temple of Amun. They were made from pink Assuan granite and gilded in gold.

Egyptian ships

The trading ships of ancient Egypt were made of short planks of wood tied together with rope around a basic wooden frame. The ships had one large linen sail and up to 16 oars on either side to propel them when the wind was light or in the wrong direction. A large oar at the back was used for steering.

The trading ships had plenty of room inside to store the items traded in Punt.

Phoenician traders

The Phoenicians, a people from Lebanon, on the east coast of the Mediterranean Sea, established colonies where they could trade with the local people. One of these colonies was Carthage in North Africa.

The voyage of Hanno

Around 475 B.C., one trader, Hanno, led a fleet of 60 ships out of Carthage to search for new places to establish colonies. They sailed out of the Mediterranean and down the coast of Africa. They may have sailed as far as Mt. Cameroon, which is the only volcano on the west coast.

DiscoveryFact™

Hanno records meeting people covered with hair, whom he called "Gorillas."

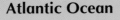

Atlantic Ocean

Pillars of Hercules

Spain

Mediterranean Sea

Carthage

Africa

The Pillars of Hercules marked the end of the known world.

Pillars of Hercules

As Hanno and his fleet headed west, they passed between the Pillars of Hercules. These two rocks are thought to have been the Rock of Gibraltar on the European coast and Mt. Hacho on the African coast.

Phoenician ships may have looked like this.

Phoenician ships

We don't know much about Phoenician trading ships. They were probably made of wood planks and powered with a single sail and rows of oars on either side.

The color purple

The Phoenicians were famous for their fine purple cloth. They extracted a liquid from sea snails to make the dye. For a pound of dye, up to 60,000 snails were needed, so purple cloth was very expensive.

Purple cloth was so rare that it was only worn by the very rich.

These ruins in present-day Tunisia are almost all that is left of the great city of Carthage.

Time Line

*c.*814 B.C.
Phoenicians establish trading city Carthage in North Africa

*c.*600 B.C.
A Phoenician ship sails around Africa

*c.*475 B.C.
Hanno sails down the west coast of Africa

Around Africa

Hanno was not the first Phoenician traveler. In around 600 B.C., the Egyptian pharaoh Necho II hired a Phoenician crew to sail down the Red Sea, around Africa, and then back through the Mediterranean to Egypt. The voyage took three years because the crew stopped each year to plant and reap a harvest of food.

China's empire

In 138 B.C., the Chinese Empire was under threat from the Huns, a nomadic tribe from central Asia. In response, the Chinese emperor Wudi sent one of his officials to seek allies among neighboring states.

The futile search

Zhang Qian set out from the Chinese capital, Chang'an, with a plan to enlist the help of the Yuezhi tribe of central Asia. But before reaching them, he was captured by the Huns and imprisoned for ten years. When he finally escaped, he traveled east to Ferghana, where he met the Yue-chi. However, they refused to fight the Huns, so Zhang Qian returned home empty-handed.

Time Line

c.160 B.C.
Birth of Zhang Qian

138–127 B.C.
Zhang Qian seeks an alliance with the Yue-chi but is imprisoned by the Huns

126 B.C.
Zhang returns home

119 B.C.
Zhang's second journey to central Asia

107 B.C.
Zhang Qian dies

c. 100 B.C.
The Silk Road opens

Black Sea

Caspian Sea

Ferghana

Kashg

Antioch

Merv

Khotan

Ecbatana

Gaofucheng

PARTHIA

INDI

Red Sea

Arabian Sea

—— **The main Silk Road**
- - - - **First journey**
- - - - **Second journey**

Han Dynasty

The Han Dynasty of emperors ruled China from 206 B.C. until A.D. 220. The emperors believed their great power came from heaven. They governed the country through a series of powerful land-owning families. They also built up a large army and extended their empire to cover much of modern-day China.

The Han made sophisticated ceramics, such as this, one of the prized Ferghana horses.

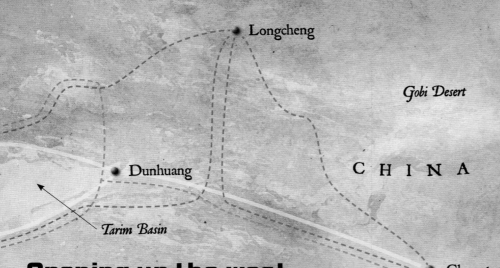

Longcheng

Gobi Desert

Dunhuang

C H I N A

Tarim Basin

Chang'an

Opening up the west

The emperor was very interested in Zhang Qian's reports of the people who lived to the west of his borders. Around 116 B.C., Wudi sent Zhang Qian back to meet these people again. This time he had more success. He made useful contacts and explored the trade routes that linked China with Kashgar and Ferghana, and south into India.

DiscoveryFact™

Zhang Qian's report to the emperor led to the opening of the Silk Road, a new trade route to Parthia and the Roman Empire. The Silk Road remained the main trade route between China and Europe for many centuries.

The Norsemen

We often think of the Norsemen, or Vikings, as savage raiders, who looted and pillaged. But the Norsemen were also intrepid travelers and traders. They were the first Europeans to visit North America.

Leif Erikson

Around A.D. 1000, Leif Erikson visited North America, sailing from Greenland down the coast of Labrador. He reached a place he named Vinland (Wine-land) because of its wild berries.

Viking ships set sail in search of adventure and new lands.

Setting sail

We are not sure why in the 9th century A.D. the Norsemen decided to leave home. However, it is likely that the growing number of younger sons with no land to inherit drove many to seek their fortune abroad. Their boats loaded up with provisions, they set out across the Atlantic Ocean.

DiscoveryFact™

By the 1400s, the climate of Greenland had become much colder, so the Vikings abandoned their settlements, leaving the island to its original Inuit inhabitants.

Norse navigation

The Norsemen found their way across the oceans using the sun and stars. By lining up a wooden bearing dial with the sun at noon, they could determine which direction was south.

One of the notches on this bearing dial points south at noon.

New world

The first Norse settlements were established in Ireland, the isles of Scotland, and the Faeroe Islands. By A.D. 870, the Norsemen had settled in Iceland. A century later, Erik the Red ventured across to Greenland, then much warmer than it is today. In A.D. 1000, the Norse leader Leif Erikson reached as far as Newfoundland, in Canada, and possibly further. A later attempt to settle the region by Thorfinn Karlsefni was unsuccessful and the Norsemen soon forgot about this new world.

Settling the new land

In 1960, a Norwegian archeologist, Helge Ingstad, discovered the foundation posts of two Norse houses at L'Anse aux Meadows, on the northern tip of Newfoundland, Canada. These houses may be the Vinland settlement, although some historians think Vinland was further down the coast, perhaps near Cape Cod.

A reconstruction of the Norse settlement at L'Anse aux Meadows.

Journey to Mecca

...least once in their lives, Muslims try ...make the hajj, or pilgrimage, to the ...cred city of Mecca in Arabia. Getting ...ere is straightforward today, but in the ...300s, this was the journey of a lifetime.

The long way around

In 1325, Ibn Battuta set off from Tangier, Morocco, to visit the holy cities of Islam. He traveled along the North African coast to Cairo and sailed up the Nile, hoping to cross overland to the Red Sea and on to Mecca. When this failed, he returned to Cairo and trekked through Palestine and Syria before reaching Mecca in 1327.

Ibn Battuta

In 1304, Ibn Battuta was born into a wealthy family of Muslim judges, so he was well educated. By the time of his death, in 1369, he had visited as many as 44 countries and traveled more than 71,500 miles.

Ancient wonder

Among the many amazing sights Ibn Battuta saw were the ruins of the Pharos lighthouse in Alexandria. One of the seven wonders of the ancient world, the lighthouse was built around 280 B.C. to guard the entrance to Alexandria.

The Pharos lighthouse, as it must once have looked.

DiscoveryFact™

Ibn Battuta wrote a chronicle of his journeys. Sometimes he exaggerated about what he saw. He claimed he saw 12,000 bishops in a cathedral in Constantinople!

Sailing south

After his hajj, Ibn Battuta decided he would visit every Muslim country in the world. He crossed the Arabian desert to Iraq and Persia before returning to Mecca, where he studied law and religion. In 1330, he traveled down the Red Sea to the coast of East Africa.

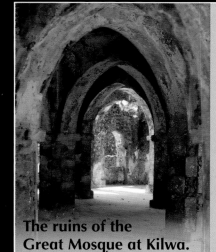

The ruins of the Great Mosque at Kilwa.

East Africa

In 1330, Ibn Battuta set out for East Africa. He visited the trading ports of Mombasa in Kenya and Kilwa in Tanzania, which he described as "one of the most beautiful and well-built of all cities." Many of the houses were built of coral and stone.

The Great Mosque in Mecca, the end point of the hajj.

Time Line

1304
Ibn Battuta born in Tangier

1325
Sets out for Cairo, and then sails up the Nile

1326
Visits Jerusalem, Damascus, and Syria

1327
Reaches Mecca, travels to Persia and Iraq

1328
Returns to Mecca

1330
Travels to East Africa, sailing as far as Kilwa

The Polos

At a time when people rarely left their home town or village, and very few ever left their own country to travel abroad, the exploits of the Polo family in the 1200s were really remarkable.

Time Line

1254
Marco Polo born in Venice

1259–69
Niccolo and Mafeo Polo make their first journey to China

1271–75
The Polos return to China with Marco

1295
The Polos arrive back in Venice

1298–99
While in prison, Marco Polo dictates *Il milione*, an account of his travels

1324
Marco Polo dies

Trading places

Niccolo and Mafeo Polo were merchants from Venice in Italy who were keen to trade with the wealthy Mongol Empire of China. In 1259, they journeyed through Russia and central Asia as far as Khanbaliq (Beijing), the capital of the Mongol Empire. Here, they met the emperor, Kublai Khan. The two brothers returned to Venice in 1269.

Kublai Khan

The Polos returned to China in 1271, this time with Niccolo's son, the 17-year-old Marco. They arrived at the summer palace of Kublai Khan (left) in Shang-du in May 1275.

Marco Polo

Marco Polo (1254–1324) was taken to China as a teenager. He worked for the Mongol emperor Kublai Khan for 20 years, becoming one of his most trusted servants. Polo spent much of this time traveling around China and Asia and learning about the region. In the 1290s, Marco returned to Venice with his father and uncle.

MONGOLIA

Gobi Desert

Kashgar

Shang-du

Bokhara

Khanbaliq (Beijing)

Khotan

Lop

The cold desert

On their way to China, the Polos crossed the bitterly cold Gobi Desert twice. Marco Polo records that they saw neither "beast nor bird," because there was nothing to eat in the desert. He also talks of mirages that played tricks with people's sight, and phantoms and evil spirits that lured travelers to their deaths. The Polos were glad to get out alive.

Kinsay (Hangzhou)

CHINA

Zaiton (Amoy)

INDIA

Indian Ocean

Bay of Bengal

South China Sea

◄---- The Polos' route to Khanbaliq (1271–75)

◄---- Marco Polo's travels while working for Kublai Khan

◄---- The Polos' route home to Venice (1292–95)

SUMATRA

BORNEO

JAVA

Zheng He's seven voyages

In 1405, Emperor Yongle ruled over the Ming Empire in China. To show his neighbors just how powerful his empire was, Yongle sent a naval expedition to sail around the region, led by the court official Zheng He.

The imperial fleet

Zheng He commanded an impressive fleet of over 300 seagoing junks. The largest was 450 feet long and had nine masts. More than 28,000 sailors were required to sail this vast fleet, which was designed to impress, not to conquer territory. When each region's ruler saw at first hand the power of the Ming Empire, he would happily acknowledge that Yongle was the most powerful emperor of all.

Time Line

1371
Zheng He born in Yunnan province

1402
Yongle becomes the third Ming emperor

1405–07
Zheng He's first voyage, to southeast Asia and India

1407–22
Zheng He makes five more voyages

1426
New emperor Xuande withdraws support from Zheng He

1433
Zheng He dies at sea during his seventh voyage

Emperor Yongle, Zhu Yuanzhang's son and the third emperor of the Ming Dynasty.

The Ming Dynasty

In 1356, the Chinese, led by a peasant and former Buddhist monk, Zhu Yuanzhang, rose up against their Mongol overlords. Zhu seized Beijing, the Mongol capital, in 1368. He declared himself Emperor Hongwu, first of the new Ming Dynasty. The Ming brought great wealth to China until they were overthrown by the Manchus in 1644.

China from China

In the mid-1300s, Chinese potters began to make pure, white porcelain decorated with bright cobalt blue. Zheng He gave porcelain to the kings he met on his travels. In return, he was given animals, such as zebras and giraffes, which he took back to the zoo in Beijing.

A late Ming Dynasty blue-and-white porcelain plate dating from the 16th century.

The Forbidden City in Beijing, built after Emperor Yongle made Beijing the Chinese capital in 1420.

The voyages

Zheng He made seven voyages between 1405 and 1433. His first three voyages took him around southeast Asia and on to India and Sri Lanka. On later voyages he reached as far west as Arabia and the east African coast. Everywhere he went, he handed out Chinese silks, porcelain, and other fine goods. In total, Zheng He visited more than 30 kingdoms. He died on a voyage around the Indian Ocean.

DiscoveryFact™

The records of Zheng He's last two voyages were destroyed. He may have visited the west coast of America and New Zealand.

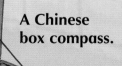

A Chinese box compass.

Pointing the way

Around A.D. 1100, the Chinese discovered that a magnetized needle always points in the same direction. They used this discovery to make a compass to help sailors find their way on their voyages.

Quick Quiz

Are these sentences TRUE or FALSE?
Place the correct sticker in the box.

1. **TRUE** The Phoenicians dyed cloth purple using snails.
2. **FALSE** The Han Dynasty of emperors were from England.
3. **TRUE** The Norsemen were the first Europeans to visit America.
4. **FALSE** Marco Polo was an American traveler.
5. **TRUE** The Chinese were the first to invent a compass.

Match the stickers to these famous explorers and rulers.

Queen Hatshepsut

Leif Erikson

Ibn Battuta

Kublai Khan

Marco Polo

ANSWERS: 1 – T, 2 – F, 3 – T, 4 – F, 5 – T

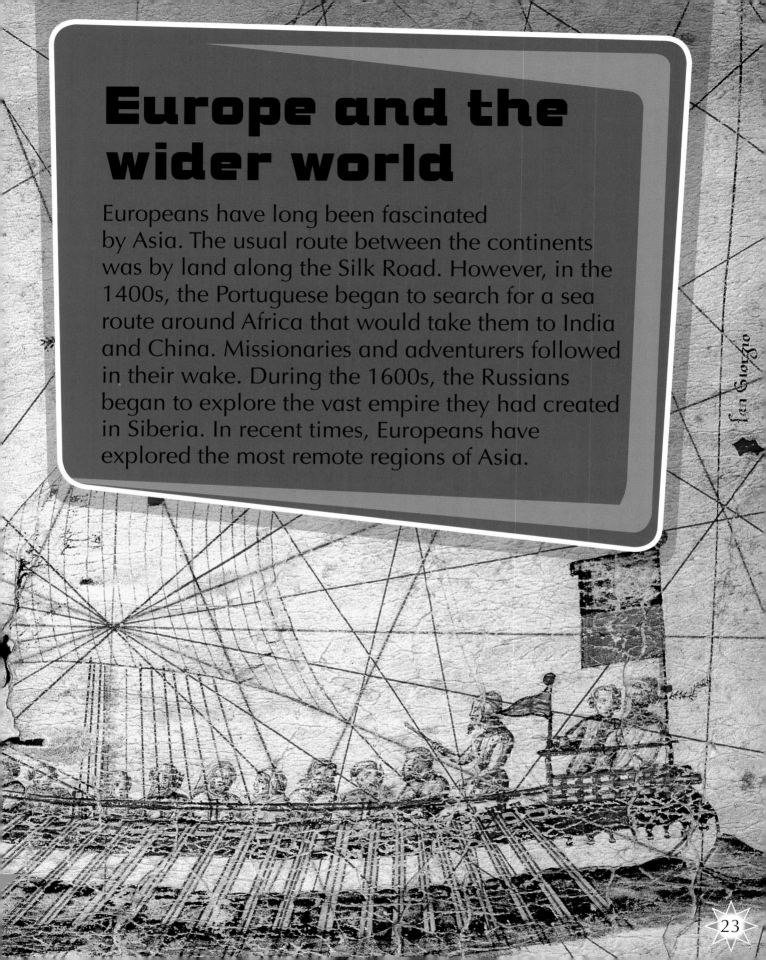

Europe and the wider world

Europeans have long been fascinated by Asia. The usual route between the continents was by land along the Silk Road. However, in the 1400s, the Portuguese began to search for a sea route around Africa that would take them to India and China. Missionaries and adventurers followed in their wake. During the 1600s, the Russians began to explore the vast empire they had created in Siberia. In recent times, Europeans have explored the most remote regions of Asia.

Prince Henry the Navigator

Henry the Navigator was a 15th-century Portuguese prince. Although he did not explore himself, it could be said that he did more for exploration than anyone before or since.

Prince Henry

Prince Henry (1394–1460) used his personal wealth to sponsor voyages, and encouraged Portuguese sailors to investigate the lands and oceans to their south.

An interest in Africa

In 1415, the Portuguese seized the city of Ceuta in Morocco from its Muslim rulers. Among the victorious army was Prince Henrique (Henry), son of King João I. The campaign inspired Henry to learn more about Africa. With his father's support, he set up a school of navigation at Sagres in southwest Portugal. From here, fleets of ships set out to explore the west African coastline.

The navigation school

Founded in 1418, the navigation school at Sagres taught mapmaking, geography, and astronomy, all essential tools for any explorer. Armed with these skills, Portuguese captains and pilots were able to map new lands so that future expeditions could benefit from their experience.

A Portuguese map from 1485, showing the west coasts of Europe and Africa.

New route to Asia

In 1453, the Portuguese voyages assumed a new urgency. The Muslim Ottoman Turks had taken the city of Constantinople and totally blocked the Silk Road from Europe to Asia. The Portuguese needed to discover a sea route around Africa that would take them to the wealth of India and China.

A drawing of a caravel from the 15th century.

The caravel

The Portuguese developed a new type of ship known as the caravel. Narrower than its predecessors, the caravel was easy to maneuver and better able to withstand storms. It had a hold under the deck in which to store the supplies necessary for a long voyage.

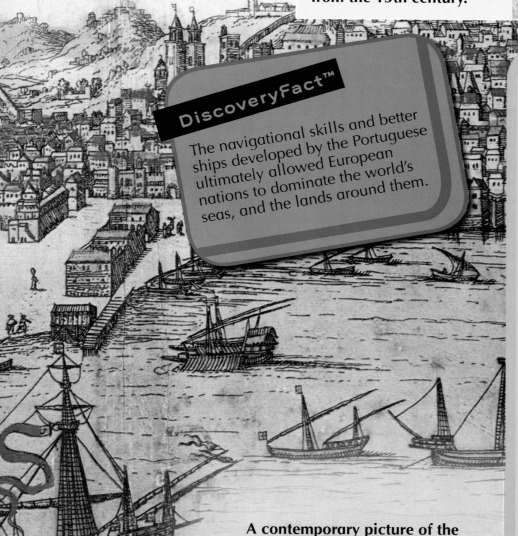

DiscoveryFact™

The navigational skills and better ships developed by the Portuguese ultimately allowed European nations to dominate the world's seas, and the lands around them.

A contemporary picture of the Portuguese capital, Lisbon.

Time Line

1415
Portuguese capture Ceuta in Africa

1418
Prince Henry founds navigation school

1427
Portuguese sailors begin exploring the west African coast

1444
Portuguese reach the Senegal River

1471
Trading post at Elmina in Ghana is established

1472
Lopo Gonçalves is first European to cross the equator

25

EUROPE

Reaching the Indian Ocean

By 1487, the Portuguese had mapped most of the west African coastline, but there appeared to be no route around it to India. One man, Bartolomeu Dias, proved this to be wrong.

The end of Africa

In 1487, Dias sailed out of Lisbon with two caravels and one supply ship. By the end of the year, he had made it south of Cape Cross. After passing the Orange River, a huge storm blew up that forced him in a southerly direction for 13 days. When it calmed, he headed east, expecting land. Instead, he found more sea.

Lisbon

- - - - - → outbound journey
- - - - - → inbound journey

Cape Verde

AFRICA

Elmina

Atlantic Ocean

Congo River

Cape Cross

Orange River

Great Fish River

The Cape of Good Hope on the southwest tip of Africa.

Cape of Good Hope

As Dias sailed west on his voyage home, he caught his first sight of the Cape of Good Hope. The name was suggested by Dias, although some historians credit King João with naming it.

Cape of Good Hope

Mossel Bay

Algoa Bay

Bartolomeu Dias

Bartolomeu Dias (c.1450–1500) added some 1,250 miles to the length of African coastline known to Europeans. After his own successful voyage, he accompanied Vasco da Gama on the first leg of his voyage to India in 1497. He was one of the commanders in Pedro Cabral's fleet that discovered Brazil in 1500. He died later in the same expedition.

Into the Indian Ocean

Dias turned north, landing at present-day Mossel Bay, 200 miles east of the Cape of Good Hope. He then sailed farther east to Algoa Bay and then on to a river he named the Rio de Infante, probably the one known today as the Great Fish River, where he erected a padrão—a large stone cross used to claim land. By now Dias was in the Indian Ocean, having rounded the southern tip of Africa. When his crew forced him to return, he sailed back west along the coast, sighting the Cape of Good Hope before he turned north to Elmina.

Indian Ocean

Time Line

1487
Dias sets sail from Lisbon with a fleet of three ships

1488
Dias is blown south by a storm and sails past the Cape of Good Hope into the Southern Ocean

1488
Dias enters Indian Ocean

1497
Dias sails with Vasco da Gama

1500
Dias sails with Cabral, discovering Brazil, then dies in a storm

The route to India

Now that Bartolomeu Dias had discovered a route around Africa into the Indian Ocean, the sea route was open to India and the east. The man to open up that route was Vasco da Gama.

Vasco da Gama

Vasco da Gama (c.1460–1524) was a ruthless Portuguese sailor whose voyage to India in 1497 opened up a new sea route to the east. Honored by King Manuel I as Admiral of India, da Gama returned in 1502 to win control over the spice trade.

Around the Cape

Da Gama set sail from Lisbon in July 1497. He stopped in the Cape Verde Islands for a week in July and then headed south into the Atlantic, away from the unpredictable winds and tides along the African coast. After 96 days he made landfall in St. Helena Bay on the west coast of South Africa. From there he edged around the Cape of Good Hope into the Indian Ocean and up the east coast of Africa to Mombasa and Malindi in Kenya.

A Portuguese map of India from the 16th century.

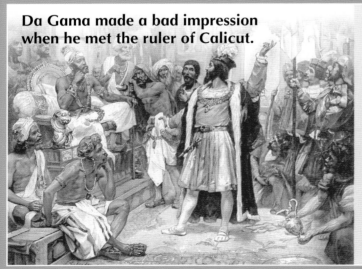

Da Gama made a bad impression when he met the ruler of Calicut.

In Calicut

Once in India, da Gama met the Hindu ruler of Calicut, but the gifts he offered him were of poor quality. The Muslims who controlled the spice trade in the region feared Portuguese intentions, and tried to get the local Hindus to destroy their fleet. Da Gama was lucky to get away.

Navigation tools

Early navigators used an astrolabe or a quadrant to work out latitude—how far north or south the ship was. The astrolabe measured the height of the sun, the quadrant the height of a star. It was not possible to measure longitude—how far east or west—accurately until the mid-18th century.

An early astrolabe, used to calculate latitude.

To India and back

Da Gama headed northeast from Malindi across the Indian Ocean. The favorable winds took him straight to Calicut in southern India, where he made landfall in May 1498. His mission accomplished, he set off home in August. His return was much harder because of unfavorable winds in the Indian Ocean, and he did not reach Lisbon until September 1499.

DiscoveryFact™

Da Gama's expedition led to the establishment of colonies in India, which remained in Portuguese hands until 1961.

Time Line

1497
Da Gama leaves Lisbon with four ships

1498
Sails up the east African coast and across the Indian Ocean to Calicut

1499
Reaches Lisbon with one ship and one fourth of his crew still alive

1502–3
Returns to India and ruthlessly enforces Portuguese control over the spice trade

1524
Da Gama dies in India

Columbus's first voyage

Italian Christopher Columbus dreamed of sailing west from Europe to reach Cipangu (Japan). In 1491, King Ferdinand and Queen Isabella of Spain agreed to fund his voyage.

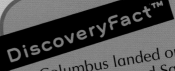

DiscoveryFact™

Columbus landed on an island he named San Salvador. Historians have suggested nine possible places in the Bahamas, but nobody really knows where Columbus landed.

The fleet

On August 3, 1492, Columbus set sail from the Spanish port of Palos with three ships: the three-masted cargo ship, *Santa María;* the three-masted caravel, the *Niña;* and the four-masted caravel, the *Pinta.* After a stop in the Canary Islands, the fleet set off again on September 6.

Columbus's fleet, the *Niña,* the *Santa María* (center), and the *Pinta.*

Columbus

Christopher Columbus (*c.*1451–1506) was born in the Italian port of Genoa. Remarkably little is know about his early life. In 1476, he moved to Lisbon and married a Portuguese noblewoman. He died in Spain in 1506.

The pineapple, one of many new foods eaten by Columbus.

New discoveries

Columbus did not find gold or rich trading cities in the lands he thought were Asia, but he and his crew did eat new foods, such as pineapples, potatoes, and corn. He also observed the Arawaks smoking tobacco leaves in a pipe.

A new world?

In the night of October 12, the lookout on the *Pinta* saw land. Columbus and crew landed on the island they named San Salvador and claimed it for Spain. Columbus was convinced he had landed off the west coast of India, so he named these islands the West Indies. He would never know he had discovered a continent that was previously unknown to Europeans.

Time Line

August 3, 1492
Columbus sets sail with three ships and a crew of 85 from Palos in Spain

October 12
Land is sighted two hours after midnight

October 28
Columbus reaches Cuba and sails along the coast before sailing to Hispaniola

December 25
While exploring the Hispaniola coastline, the Santa María runs aground and is abandoned

January 16, 1493
After establishing a colony in what is now Haiti, Columbus returns to Spain

The Arawaks

On San Salvador, Columbus traded glass beads with the native Arawaks in return for parrots and "a kind of dry leaf," tobacco. The Arawaks told him of a king to the south who had much gold, and Columbus set off to find him. The Arawaks soon died of diseases brought by Europeans, for which they had no immunity.

Arawak musicians danced as they played.

Columbus returns

After his first voyage in 1492–93, Columbus crossed the Atlantic Ocean three more times to explore the islands he had first visited. These voyages opened up the new continent to European explorers and conquerors.

Time Line

1493–96
On his second voyage, Columbus explores and names the Leeward Islands, and establishes a colony on Hispaniola

July 31, 1498
On his third voyage, Columbus lands on Trinidad before exploring mainland South America nearby

August 19, 1498
Returns to Hispaniola, where he is placed under arrest and then sent home

1502–4
Explores east coast of Central America, searching for a passage to the Indian Ocean

1506
Columbus dies

DiscoveryFact™

In 1494, Pope Alexander VI signed the Treaty of Tordesillas. He drew a line down a map of the Atlantic Ocean and divided the New World between the Spanish and Portuguese.

Around the Caribbean

In 1493–96, Columbus made his second voyage, exploring the Caribbean and establishing a settlement on Hispaniola. On his third voyage in 1498, he became the first European to set foot on South America. He then returned to rule Santo Domingo. Following complaints, he was arrested by the new Spanish governor and sent to Spain for trial.

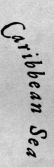

Caribbean Sea

New settlers

The first Spanish settlements in the New World were established on the island of Hispaniola. The first colony, La Navidad, was destroyed by local Taíno people. Columbus set up a new colony at Santo Domingo, which is now the capital of the Dominican Republic.

A reconstructed Taíno village on Hispaniola.

Farther west

Columbus won his trial in Spain, and in 1502 he set out again. This time he headed west through the islands until he hit land. This was the Central American coastline, but Columbus thought he had found a route through to Asia.

CUBA

La Navidad

HISPANIOLA

Santo Domingo

North Atlantic Ocean

JAMAICA

LEEWARD ISLANDS

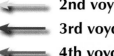

← **2nd voyage (1493–96)**

← **3rd voyage (1498–1500)**

← **4th voyage (1502–4)**

The Spanish Empire

The Spanish were very cruel to the native population, who rebelled against their rule. This, combined with new diseases, completely wiped out the native population of the Caribbean.

Hatuey, a Taíno leader, fought Spanish rule on Cuba and was burned alive after refusing to be baptized.

TRINIDAD

SOUTH AMERICA

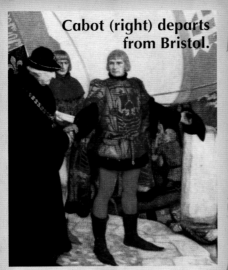

Cabot (right) departs from Bristol.

John Cabot

John Cabot, or Giovanni Caboto, was born in Italy in about 1450 and died around 1498. He settled in Bristol, England, where he hoped to find sponsors for his voyage. His son, Sebastian (1476–1557), was also a noted explorer.

Newfoundland

When Columbus returned to Europe in 1493 with news of his "discovery" of a new route to Asia, other navigators quickly followed him. Italian sailor John Cabot decided to sail a shorter route.

Sailing north

Spices arriving in England via the Middle East were very expensive, so merchants were interested in finding a shorter route to the east. Cabot knew that the shortest route to Asia would be to sail across the Atlantic Ocean at the most northern latitude as possible. He presented his proposals to Henry VII of England.

The Newfoundland coast, where Cabot probably landed in 1497.

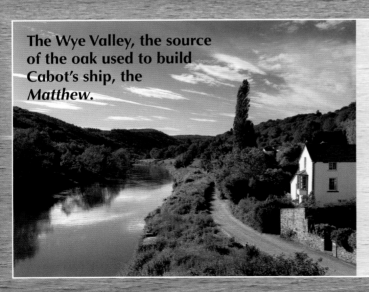

The Wye Valley, the source of the oak used to build Cabot's ship, the *Matthew.*

A wealthy sponsor

Richard Amerike was a wealthy Welsh merchant who became Sheriff of Bristol in 1503. Amerike sponsored Cabot's two voyages, and some historians believe that Cabot named the new lands he found after his generous sponsor.

Canadian landfall

Henry VII agreed to support the voyage, so in 1497 Cabot set off from Bristol onboard the *Matthew*. He landed in North America, probably on the island of Newfoundland, or possibly farther south at Nova Scotia, both in modern-day Canada. In 1498, Cabot set off again, this time with five ships, but was never heard of again.

The replica of the *Matthew*.

The *Matthew*

Cabot's boat, the *Matthew,* was a three-masted ship. It weighed about 55 tons, making it a relatively small ship. Built of oak, it carried a crew of about 18 sailors and, although small, was very seaworthy. In 1997, a replica was built in Bristol to celebrate the 500th anniversary of the *Matthew*'s voyage.

Time Line

1494 or 1495
Cabot settles in Bristol

May 1497
Cabot sails west

June 24, 1497
Makes landfall in either Newfoundland or Nova Scotia

August 6 1497
Returns to Bristol

May 1498
Cabot sets out on his second voyage and is never heard of again

DiscoveryFact™

Cabot thought he had landed on an island off the coast of Asia. By 1502, it was called "the newfound land," and the name is still used for the Canadian province of Newfoundland.

Naming the continent

Although Columbus was convinced he had sailed to the "Indies," or Asia, others were unsure because the land was too close to Europe to be Asia. It was, in fact, a new continent previously unknown to Europeans.

Who was first?

In 1499–1500, four Europeans sailed to South America. Who arrived first is unclear, although many historians credit Pedro Cabral, who sighted Brazil on April 22, 1500. Vicente Pinzón reached the northeast of Brazil, possibly in January 1500. On a third expedition, Alonso de Ojeda explored the Caribbean coast, and Amerigo Vespucci sailed along the coast farther east.

Amerigo Vespucci

Amerigo Vespucci (1451–1512) was born in Florence in northern Italy. In 1491, Vespucci left for Seville in Spain, and in 1499, he joined the expedition led by Alonso de Ojeda (c.1468–1515).

Time Line

1499–1500
Ojeda sails along the Caribbean coast; Vespucci explores eastern Brazil

1500
Vicente Pinzón and Pedro Cabral land in Brazil

1501–02
Vespucci makes second voyage possibly reaching as far south as Patagonia in modern-day Argentina

DiscoveryFact™

Portugal's territory in the new continent was named "Brasil," after a term used by Irish monks and seafarers for a legendary unknown land.

The Amazon estuary seen from space.

Amerigo's land

In 1501–02, Vespucci made a second voyage down the east coast of South America. He was convinced that this was a new continent, which he called the New World. His account of his travels was really popular, and his new world was known as "the land of Amerigo," or America (a term initially applied only to South America).

Mercator's map of 1538, the first to name both American continents. It shows North and South America, with the Atlantic Ocean to the east and the Pacific Ocean to the west.

Father of Brazil

In April 1500, Pedro Cabral (c.1467–c.1520) "accidentally discovered" Brazil. Whether he was the first European or not, Brazilians celebrate Cabral as the discoverer of their country.

Cabral's caravel.

The Amazon

As Vicente Pinzón (1463–1514) headed northeast up the coast of Brazil, he noticed that the water had changed color and was no longer salty. He had discovered the estuary of the mighty Amazon River.

The impossible voyage

Ferdinand Magellan didn't mean to sail around the world and, in fact, he didn't, because he died halfway around. But his voyage is forever associated with the first circumnavigation of the world and was a remarkable feat of exploration.

A new route to Asia

Magellan set out to do what Columbus had tried 27 years earlier—sailing west to find a sea route to Asia. With five Spanish ships, he set out in 1519 in search of the Spice Islands in Indonesia. He sailed south down the Atlantic, then wintered in Patagonia (southern Argentina).

An old map showing the Strait of Magellan, at the tip of South America, which connects the Atlantic and Pacific oceans.

Ferdinand Magellan

Magellan (c.1480–1521) was born in Portugal. He moved to Spain in 1517 to work for the Spanish king. Magellan was a skilled navigator and leader, demanding much of his men and even more of himself.

Battle of Mactan

In the Philippines, Magellan tried to convert the local chiefs to Christianity. When the chief of Mactan refused, Magellan attempted to punish him. Magellan was killed when the chief and his army attacked him and his men.

Magellan was killed by blows to the arm and the right leg.

Guam

The island of Guam is one of the Mariana Islands. The Spanish called the islands the Ladrones, the Spanish word for "thieves," because the islanders stole everything they could. But they gave Magellan fresh water, coconuts, and rice to feed his crew.

Guam is dotted with these "latte" stones—the remains of ancient houses.

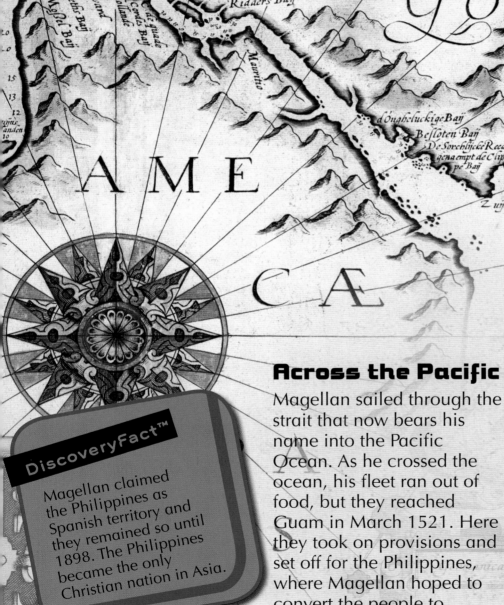

DiscoveryFact™

Magellan claimed the Philippines as Spanish territory and they remained so until 1898. The Philippines became the only Christian nation in Asia.

Across the Pacific

Magellan sailed through the strait that now bears his name into the Pacific Ocean. As he crossed the ocean, his fleet ran out of food, but they reached Guam in March 1521. Here they took on provisions and set off for the Philippines, where Magellan hoped to convert the people to Christianity. He was killed the following month.

Time Line

September 10, 1519
Magellan sets sail from Spain with five ships

March/April 1520
Winters in Patagonia and puts down a revolt by one of his captains

November 1520
Sails through the Strait of Magellan into the Pacific Ocean

March 6, 1521
Reaches Guam

March 16, 1521
Arrives in the Philippines

March 28, 1521
Magellan's servant talks to the locals in his own language, proving to Magellan that he had reached Asia

April 27, 1521
Magellan killed on Mactan Island

The voyage home

Soon after Magellan's death, the remaining voyagers elected João Lopes Carvalho as their leader. Carvalho burned one of the three ships, destroyed Magellan's records, and for the next four months raided any passing ship for loot.

The *Victoria,* the only ship to make it home.

The new leader

Juan Sebastián Delcano (c.1492–1526) was the Basque seaman who completed Magellan's voyage. He showed that travelers who sailed west around the world lost a day by the time they came home, due to the rotation of the Earth.

Homeward bound

When Carvalho failed to find the Spice Islands, command was given to Juan Delcano. He discovered the spice-rich islands and then sailed home west to Spain. On board the *Victoria,* Delcano reached Spain in September 1522. With him were only 17 out of the original 250 European men, plus four East Indians.

DiscoveryFact™

When Magellan came out of the Strait of Magellan into the new ocean, he found it to be "calm and benevolent," so he named it the Pacific Ocean.

Atlantic Ocean

EURO

Spain

AFRICA

Pacific Ocean

SOUTH AMERICA

Strait of Magellan

The great voyage

Although he did not live to enjoy it, Magellan's voyage was a huge achievement. He had discovered a westerly route to Asia and sailed across the Pacific Ocean, showing Europeans just how big the world was. He had also opened up new trade possibilities in the Philippines and Spice Islands, as well as discovering a whole new world of Pacific islands to be explored— and exploited—by Europeans.

Spices such as these were widely available in Asia.

Spice trade

Spices were highly valued in Europe for flavoring meat, after it had been salted, to preserve it. They were also used to flavor drinks. Among those found in the Spice Islands were pepper, cloves, and nutmeg.

Time Line

May 1521
Carvalho is elected leader a few days after Magellan is killed in battle

October 1521
After failing to find the Spice Islands, the remaining crew get rid of Carvalho and give command to Delcano

November 1521
Delcano finds the Spice Islands and sails for home in the *Victoria*, leaving the *Trinidad* behind for repairs

April 1522
The *Trinidad* returns to the Spice Islands and is held captive by the Portuguese

September 6, 1522
Delcano reaches Spain

Indian Ocean

Magellan killed

Philippines

Pacific Ocean

Spice Islands

Southern Ocean

Cortés in Mexico

The people that explorers first encountered in the Americas were self-sufficient farmers and hunters. In European eyes, they were very primitive, but this view of the continent changed when the Aztec Empire of Mexico was discovered.

Into the interior

In 1518, the Spanish governor of Cuba sent 11 ships under the command of Hernán Cortés (1485–1547) to explore the coast of the Yucatán peninsula of Mexico. Once there, Cortés learned of a great inland empire and set out to find it. He marched inland with only a handful of men and horses, but soon found local allies willing to fight against their rulers, the Aztecs.

An Aztec map of Tenochtitlán.

Tenochtitlán

The Aztec capital housed perhaps 250,000 people—far more than any European city of the time. It ruled an empire of 10 million people from the Pacific to the Caribbean.

An Aztec calendar, based on a complex cycle of 20-day periods.

The Aztecs

The Aztecs settled in central Mexico in the 13th century and soon created a powerful empire. They developed a complex calendar and built vast cities of stone. Yet they had no iron tools, wheeled vehicles, or horses.

A mighty empire falls

Cortés entered the Aztec capital, Tenochtitlán, and took the emperor, Moctezuma II, hostage. Cortés was then forced to return to the coast to deal with charges of insubordination, and left the city in the charge of his lieutenant, Pedro de Alvarado. On his return, Cortés found that Alvarado had massacred a group of Aztec nobles. In response, the Aztecs revolted, killed Moctezuma, and forced the Spanish to flee. A year later, Cortés seized Tenochtitlán and took control of the entire Aztec Empire.

The city of Tenochtitlán, built on an island in Lake Texcoco.

Moctezuma II

The Aztec emperor Moctezuma II (reigned 1502–20) was portrayed as a weak leader in Spanish accounts. Before losing to Cortés, however, he had many military successes and conquered large parts of southern Mexico.

Time Line

November 18, 1518
Cortés leads an expedition from Cuba with 900 men

August 16, 1519
Cortés moves inland

November 1519
Cortés enters Tenochtitlán and takes the Aztec emperor, Moctezuma II, hostage

December 1519
The Aztecs revolt when Cortés is out of the city

June 30–July 1, 1520
Cortés fights his way out of Tenochtitlán, losing half his men

May–August 1521
The Spanish and their allies attack and seize Tenochtitlán

DiscoveryFact™

Tenochtitlán was not the first important city in the Valley of Mexico. The great city of Teotihuacán stood nearby many centuries earlier. The huge, sprawling Mexico City still stands there today.

In search of the Incas

Rumors circulated in the New World of a gold-rich civilization known as Birù (or Peru) on the Pacific coast of South America. One man set out to look for this legendary civilization.

Francisco Pizarro

Pizarro (c.1475–1541) served as a soldier with Balboa in 1513 before becoming a cattle breeder in Panama. When he set out to conquer the Inca Empire in 1530, he was about 55. This was his last chance for glory.

Head for the hills

Spanish explorer Francisco Pizarro led three expeditions to find Birù. The first found nothing. The second, in 1526, sailed as far south as the Inca city of Tumbes in northern Peru. It returned with news of an advanced civilization up in the mountains. Pizarro set out in 1530 to conquer it.

The Inca Empire

The Inca Empire stretched the length of South America from Ecuador in the north to central Chile in the south and across the Andes to Argentina in the east. The empire was connected by a vast network of paved roads.

An Inca headdress, one of many objects the Incas made from gold.

Seizing Cusco

Pizarro and his party made their way south to Tumbes, which they now found in ruins following a civil war in the Inca Empire. With fewer than 200 men, Pizarro set out to meet the emperor, Atahuallpa. He took the emperor hostage and was offered a room full of gold and silver to release him. But when this treasure was handed over, Pizarro executed the emperor and seized the capital, Cusco. The Inca Empire was his.

Machu Picchu, a royal Inca retreat in the mountains of Peru, was abandoned by the Incas after the Spanish conquest and remained unknown to the outside world until 1911.

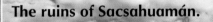

The ruins of Sacsahuamán.

Sacsahuamán fortress

This was the main Inca fortress guarding the capital, Cusco. It was a vast stone building with three massive terraced walls, capable of housing 5,000 soldiers. Inca stonemasons cut and shaped each stone individually.

Time Line

1524–25
Pizarro finds no gold on first voyage south

1526–28
Sails south to Tumbes, where he hears of a city in the mountains

May 1532
Returns to Tumbes, which he finds in ruins

November 1532
Heads inland to Cajamarca, where he takes Atahuallpa hostage

July 1533
Atahuallpa is executed

November 1533
Pizarro's army take the Inca capital Cusco

DiscoveryFact™

The last Inca stronghold fell to the Spanish in 1572, but the edges of the empire remained largely unconquered until the early 1800s.

45

Into Canada

While the Spanish explored Central America and Florida, the French concentrated on what is now Canada. They hoped to find a waterway through North America that would take them to Asia. What they discovered instead became the basis of a vast empire in the Americas.

First steps

In 1534, Jacques Cartier (1491–1557) set out to find a northwest passage to Asia. He sailed into the Gulf of St. Lawrence, and returned the following year and discovered the mighty St. Lawrence River—the gateway into Canada. Cartier sailed up the river, stopping at Stadacona (modern Québec) and Hochelaga. He named the hill near Hochelaga Mont Réal (Mount Royal), modern-day Montréal.

Sir Walter Raleigh

English adventurer Walter Raleigh (c.1552–1618) led an expedition in 1584 to set up an English colony in North America. The colony that he founded at Roanoke in North Carolina lasted only a year.

DiscoveryFact™

In 1587, 100 English settlers under Governor John White arrived on Roanoke Island. White returned to England for supplies, but when he came back in 1590, all the settlers had vanished without a trace.

St. Lawrence River

Jacques Cartier found it impossible to sail up the St. Lawrence River and its tributaries because of the many white-water rapids above Montréal. Samuel de Champlain solved this problem by copying the locals and traveling by canoe.

The Hochelaga negotiated rapids in canoes.

French settlers

French fur trappers, traders, and fishermen followed Cartier to Canada, but it was not until the next century that an attempt was made to settle the area permanently. Samuel de Champlain (1567–1635) established Québec—one of the first French settlements in Canada. In 1615, he explored Lake Ontario.

Woodland around the Great Lakes in dazzling fall splendor.

First nations

The French got along well with the native people, and used them as guides. De Champlain sided with the Algonquins, Hurons, and Montagnais against the Iroquois, who later helped the British throw the French out of Canada.

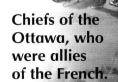

Chiefs of the Ottawa, who were allies of the French.

Time Line

1534
Cartier explores the coast of Newfoundland

1535–36
Travels up St. Lawrence River to Montréal

1587
English colonists settle on Roanoke Island, but have all gone by 1590

1603
De Champlain explores the St. Lawrence up to Montréal

1608–9
Founds Québec

1615–16
Rows up Ottawa River by canoe, crosses overland to Lakes Ontario and Oneida

The Mississippi

By the late 17th century, Europeans had successfully founded colonies in the south, east, and north of North America. But the interior of the continent remained relatively unknown to them. That changed after two extraordinary journeys by French explorers.

·The new river

In 1673, fur trader Louis Jolliet (1645–1700), Jesuit priest Jacques Marquette (1637–75), and five others set out from the north to explore a great inland river they had heard about. They canoed down the Wisconsin River into the Mississippi, which they paddled down for more than 1,000 miles until they met hostile Quapaw people and turned back. The Quapaw had Spanish goods, which suggested that the river emptied into the Gulf of Mexico, where the Spanish had set up colonies.

Cavelier de La Salle

René Robert Cavelier de La Salle (1643–87) was the son of a rich merchant from Rouen in France. He was training to become a priest before choosing a life of adventure and moving to the New World or the Americas.

This print shows Jolliet and Marquette being paddled down the Mississippi by Illinois allies.

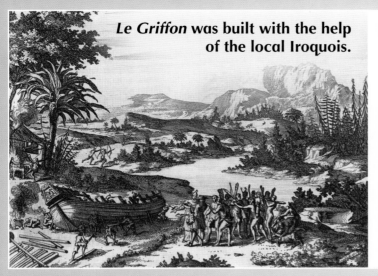

Le Griffon was built with the help of the local Iroquois.

Building *Le Griffon*

In 1678, La Salle built a ship, *Le Griffon*, at Niagara. It was the first full-size sailing ship on the Great Lakes. He built it to carry the furs he was hoping would pay for his expedition down the river. *Le Griffon* sailed through the Great Lakes and was soon laden with furs, but it sank on its way back to Niagara and the valuable cargo was lost.

Time Line

May 17, 1673
Jolliet and Marquette cross Lake Michigan and paddle into the Mississippi

July 17, 1673
The expedition meets Quapaw people and turns back near the Arkansas River

1678
La Salle sets up headquarters at Niagara on the Great Lakes

December 21, 1681
La Salle sets off for the Mississippi

April 6, 1682
La Salle reaches the delta; the party splits into three and meets three days later in the Gulf of Mexico

All the way down

In 1681, La Salle set off to explore the Mississippi River. Approaching the Mississippi via the Illinois River, the expedition canoed south until they, too, met the Quapaw near the Arkansas River. This time, the Quapaw allowed the party to continue south. In April 1682, the expedition reached the Mississippi Delta and the sea. The center of North America was now open to exploration and colonial settlement.

DiscoveryFact™

La Salle claimed the Mississippi basin for France, naming it Louisiana for the king, Louis XIV. This territory remained French until 1763. It was sold to the United States in 1803.

Mississippi Delta

When La Salle's expedition reached the delta at the mouth of the Mississippi, they split up to explore the vast marshes. The city of New Orleans was founded in 1718 to take advantage of the area's natural resources.

The Mississippi Delta seen from space.

New frontier

In 1803, President Thomas Jefferson bought territory west of the Mississippi River from the French for $15 million. Jefferson commissioned an expedition to find out exactly what it was he had bought.

Heading west

The expedition was led by Jefferson's secretary, Meriwether Lewis, and his friend, William Clark. They were told to explore the newly acquired territory and to find a route through it to the Pacific coast. In May 1804, the pair set off from St. Louis on the banks of the Mississippi and canoed up the Missouri River toward the Rocky Mountains.

Lewis and Clark

Meriwether Lewis (1774–1809), pictured left, and William Clark (1770–1838), right, met while they were serving in the army. In 1803, Lewis asked Clark to become co-leader of the Corps of Discovery, as the expedition was known. The pair worked very well with each other. Lewis was very good at organization, while Clark had vast experience in survival techniques and was a skilled mapmaker. They shared leadership duties, but Clark was the main guide through the dangerous Rockies.

Unlike other Plains Indians, the Mandan lived in permanent villages, such as this one, where the men are performing a bull dance.

Friendly locals

Lewis and Clark spent their first winter with the Mandan, a friendly tribe of hunters and farmers. While there, they were approached by a Montréal fur trapper, Toussaint Charbonneau, who wished to join the expedition. His wife Sacajawea was a Shoshone Indian. She proved invaluable as an interpreter and helped the expedition through potentially hostile territory.

DiscoveryFact™

In August 1805, the expedition made first contact with the Shoshone tribe. Their Shoshone guide, Sacajawea, took them to meet the tribe, and recognized its chief as her long-lost brother.

Crossing the Rockies

The expedition rode on horseback through the Rockies. They then paddled down toward the Columbia River. They reached the Pacific coast in November 1805. The route they had found to the Pacific was not easy. During their journey, however, they had made friendly contact with many tribes and found out a lot about this vast territory.

The Rocky Mountains lay across the route to the Pacific Ocean, and were very difficult to cross.

Hostile territory

The expedition faced many challenges while crossing the Rockies. Grizzly bears constantly attacked them, and at one point chased six men into the river. On another occasion a buffalo charged straight through their camp.

Grizzly bears are a constant threat in the Rockies.

Quick Quiz

Are these sentences TRUE or FALSE?
Place the correct sticker in the box.

1. FALSE The navigation school was founded in 1914.
2. TRUE Bartolomeu Dias was a famous Portugese explorer.
3. TRUE Christopher Columbus discovered the West Indies.
4. There is a replica of Cabot's boat, the Matthew, in England.
5. The city of New Orleans was founded in 1718.

Match the stickers to these famous explorers and rulers.

Prince Henry

Bartolomeu Dias

Christopher Columbus

John Cabot

Sir Walter Raleigh

ANSWERS: 1 – F, 2 – T, 3 – T, 4 – T, 5 – T

Into the unknown

Although Magellan had crossed the Pacific Ocean during his circumnavigation, little was known about this vast ocean. Over the years, European navigators slowly mapped the Pacific, eventually discovering a new continent as well as many new islands. Meanwhile, Europeans knew nothing of the interior of Africa and its many kingdoms, and even less about its great rivers that could lead them into the interior. In the late 18th century, they set out to explore this unknown continent.

The incredible Polynesians

Long before Europeans arrived in the Pacific Ocean, navigators had already explored the ocean and colonized its many islands. Their perilous voyages are among the most remarkable human expeditions of all time.

A Polynesian double canoe, similar in design to a modern-day catamaran.

Who were they?

The first inhabitants of the Pacific islands moved east from Indonesia in around 2000 B.C., reaching Fiji, Tonga, and Samoa by 1000 B.C. Here, they developed a distinctive Polynesian culture. In about 200 B.C., they began to seek new islands, sailing east to Tahiti and Easter Island, and north, to what is today known as Hawaii, then south to Aotearoa (New Zealand).

DiscoveryFact™

When Captain Cook measured a Maori canoe in Aotearoa in 1770, he found it was longer than the ship he was sailing.

The Maori

Aotearoa was the last island group to be colonized. The Maori, as the new settlers were known, adapted their customs to live off the islands' unique animals and plants.

A Maori man with traditional facial tattoos.

More than 800 of these giant statues stand on Easter Island. Nobody knows why they were made.

Easter Island

Easter Island is more than 1,000 miles from its nearest island neighbor and is so remote that the islanders believed they were the only people on the Earth. They were the only Polynesians to develop a form of writing.

Navigation techniques

The Polynesians had no instruments to guide them. Instead, they navigated by observing changes in the wind and currents, looking at wave patterns, and following migrating birds. They also used the sun and stars. Each island had its "on top" star, so that when, for example, Sirius was overhead, they knew they were in the same latitude as Tahiti. Using these simple methods, they colonized the entire Pacific Ocean.

Stick charts

Polynesian navigators were trained using a stick chart, such as this one from the Marshall Islands. The charts were made of a network of palm sticks tied together with coconut fiber. Shells threaded onto the sticks marked the position of each island relative to the ocean currents, allowing a navigator to learn the geography of the region.

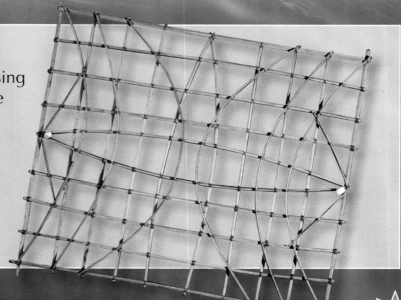

Around Australia

In two epic voyages, the Dutch explorer Abel Tasman sailed around Australia and explored its northern coast. Despite proving that this new continent was not part of a larger southern continent, his expeditions were considered a failure.

New Guinea

Batavia

Torres Strait

Pacific Ocean

→ **First expedition (1642–43)**

← **Second expedition (1644)**

Australia

Abel Tasman

Abel Tasman (1603–59) was born in Lutjegast, Holland. In 1634, he moved to Batavia (now Jakarta) on Java, where he was employed as a captain by the Dutch East India Company. After his voyages, he became a judge in Batavia.

DiscoveryFact™

The Dutch never publicized Tasman's voyages, because they did not want anyone else to know about the newly discovered lands in the Pacific.

Van Diemen's Land

South of the continent

In 1642, Tasman sailed west from Batavia across the Indian Ocean to Mauritius. His mission was to explore the land south of Java and find a passage between the Indian and Pacific oceans to lead Dutch sailors to the riches of South America. From Mauritius, Tasman sailed south and east, becoming the first European to visit Tasmania (which he named Van Diemen's Land), New Zealand, and Fiji. The voyage took him all the way around Australia, and proved conclusively that it was not the fabled "Great South Land."

Exploration

For his second voyage, Tasman attempted to establish the relationships of New Guinea, Australia, the new Van Diemen's Land, and the "unknown South Land" (Antarctica). However, he failed to recognize the Torres Strait, and returned to Batavia after sailing along Australia's north coast.

Tasman Sea

New Zealand

Time Line

August 14, 1642
Tasman sets sail from Batavia to find a shortcut to Chile and explore the "Great South Land"

December 13, 1642
Sights South Island of New Zealand, which he believes to be part of the southern continent; mistakes strait between the islands for a bay

April 1643
Discovers Fiji

February 29, 1644
Sets sail for New Guinea and Australia via the Torres Strait, which he mistakes for a bay; explores north coast of Australia then returns to Batavia

Dutch East Indies

The Dutch East India Company was set up in 1602 to challenge Spanish and Portuguese control of the spice trade. Basing itself in Batavia, its large fleet of ships quickly gained control of many of the seas around southeast Asia.

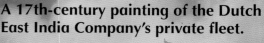

A 17th-century painting of the Dutch East India Company's private fleet.

The first voyage of Captain Cook

Despite many voyages across the Pacific, the ocean remained largely unknown to Europeans well into the 18th century. So the quest for the great southern continent remained as intense as ever.

Circling New Zealand

In 1768, the Royal Society, a body set up in Great Britain to promote science, asked James Cook to supervise an expedition to Tahiti. They wanted him to observe the path of the planet Venus across the sun. The British Admiralty supported the expedition, hoping to discover the great southern continent. Cook arrived in the south Pacific in April 1769 and sailed around both islands of New Zealand, proving they were not part of a larger continent.

Time Line

August 26, 1768
Cook leaves Plymouth, England; collects plant specimens on Tierra del Fuego

April 13, 1769
Anchors off Tahiti for three months

October 1769
Reaches New Zealand and sails around the two islands

April 29, 1770
Lands at Botany Bay

October 1770
Sails up west coast of Australia, around northern tip, and reaches Batavia via the Torres Strait

Captain James Cook

James Cook (1728–79) was born in Yorkshire, England, the son of a poor farmer. He first went to sea at the age of 14 to work on a coal ship. He joined the Royal Navy in 1755, and quickly worked his way up through the ranks. His navigational skills and experience of observing eclipses made him the ideal person to lead the three missions to the South Seas.

The *Endeavour*

The *Endeavour* was a converted coal ship similar to the ones Cook sailed in when he first went to sea. The ship was not elegant or fast but it was large. It was roomy enough to accommodate a crew of 94 men plus their provisions, and tough enough for the long voyage.

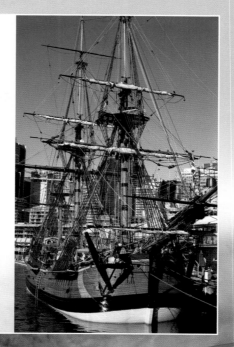

A replica of the *Endeavour* in Whitby, Yorkshire, England.

First landing

Cook sailed west across the Tasman Sea, sighting land on the southeast coast of Australia at Point Hicks on April 19. Ten days later he landed at Botany Bay. Continuing northward, Cook ran aground on the Great Barrier Reef and was forced to land to make repairs. He then sailed to Batavia via the Torres Strait before returning home.

DiscoveryFact™

When Cook's crew first saw a kangaroo, they were unsure what type of animal it was. The size of a deer, but jumping like a hare, they decided it must be a "kind of stag."

Cook's crew were the first Europeans to see kangaroos, such as this one.

New discoveries

Naturalists Joseph Banks and Daniel Solander were onboard the *Endeavour*, along with painter Sydney Parkinson. Together, they recorded many new exotic plants, animals, and insects.

A drawing by Sydney Parkinson of red honeysuckle.

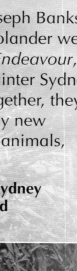

Discovering Antarctica

For his second expedition, Cook was sent on a final search for the legendary southern continent. The British Admiralty was still not sure whether the southern continent really existed.

Crossing the Circle

Cook sailed south down the Atlantic Ocean until he crossed the Antarctic Circle—he was the first explorer to do so. He then sailed through the Southern Ocean to New Zealand and took on more supplies before heading south again. The mythical continent was thought to lie somewhere between New Zealand and Cape Horn.

Time Line

July 13, 1772
Cook sets sail with two ships in search of the southern continent

January 17, 1773
Crosses Antarctic Circle and sails to New Zealand for supplies

November 1774
Sailing south to Antarctica, Cook's two ships are separated; the *Adventure* returns to England

December 1774
The *Resolution* is surrounded by icebergs

July 29, 1775
Having survived the winter, Cook returns home via Cape Horn

A drawing from 1809 of the *Resolution* surrounded by packed ice off Antarctica.

The *Resolution*

Cook made his second voyage with the *Resolution* and the *Adventure*. They were both converted coal ships, whose strong hulls protected them from icebergs. The *Resolution* was originally named the *Drake,* after explorer and pirate Sir Francis Drake, but this was changed to avoid upsetting the Spanish.

Cook attends a village meeting on Tahiti.

Tahiti

On each of his voyages, Cook stopped off in Tahiti. When he saw that Tahitians and Easter Islanders could understand each other, he began to suspect that South Sea islanders all shared a common ancestry.

The southern continent

Finding only a few small islands, Cook returned to New Zealand before sailing south again. He crossed the Antarctic Circle twice more before icebergs forced him north. Having sailed right around the South Pole, he could rule out the existence of a massive continent. However, he believed that he had found a large piece of land near the Pole.

The coastline of Antarctica, which Cook believed he saw.

DiscoveryFact™

After his second voyage, Cook wrote a report on how to prevent scurvy, a potentially fatal disease caused by a lack of vitamin C.

Sea chronometer

Until Cook's time, navigators had been able to calculate latitude (position north–south) but not longitude (east–west). In 1760, John Harrison developed the chronometer for accurately measuring longitude. Cook used this on his second voyage.

The H5, one of Harrison's chronometers.

Cook's final voyage

On his final voyage, Cook set out to find the northwest passage between the Atlantic and Pacific oceans. Two other expeditions searched for a passage from the Atlantic side, while Cook looked for one from the Pacific.

Finding Hawaii

Setting sail with both the *Resolution* and the *Discovery*, Cook left England in July 1776. He sailed south to Cape Town and then across the Indian Ocean to New Zealand. He revisited Tahiti, and what are now known as the Cook Islands. He then sailed north, finding the previously unknown volcanic Hawaiian Islands, which he named the Sandwich Isles.

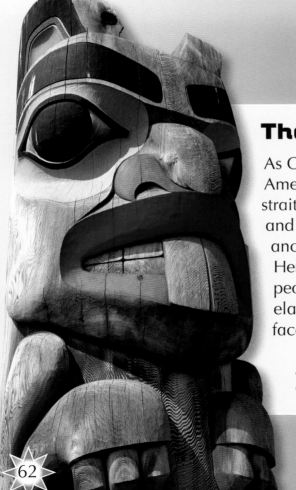

The NuuChahNulth

As Cook sailed up the American coast, he missed the strait between Vancouver Island and the mainland, and anchored in Nootka Sound. Here, the local NuuChahNulth people greeted him wearing elaborate masks and painted faces.

A NuuChahNulth totem pole carved from a cedar tree.

Time Line

July 12, 1776
Cook sets sail from Plymouth, England.

January 1777
Heads to New Zealand and on to Tahiti and the Cook Islands

December 1777
Lands on an island he calls Christmas Island

January 1778
Reaches Hawaii, then cruises up the North American coastline

August 18, 1778
Becomes icebound in the Arctic Ocean and heads south again

January 17, 1779
Returns to Hawaii

February 14, 1779
Cook is killed on Hawaii Island

The Aleutian Islands

The Aleutian Islands stretch from southwest Alaska along the south of the Bering Sea. Vitus Bering was the first to explore the islands in 1741. Cook sailed along the eastern end of the chain before he headed north into the Bering Sea.

Cook's final days

In spring and summer 1778, Cook explored the North American coast from Oregon north to Alaska. He sailed down the Aleutian Islands before turning north again into the Bering Sea. He became increasingly unsure that he would find the passage. When ice surrounded his ships, he headed back to Hawaii, where he was killed on February 14, 1779.

Mauna Kea is the largest of five volcanoes on Hawaii Island.

DiscoveryFact™

Among the crew of the *Resolution* was William Bligh. Years later, in 1787, he was made captain of HMS *Bounty*. His crew mutinied and set Bligh and 18 others adrift in a small boat.

The Death of Cook

Cook tried to deal fairly with the people he met. In Hawaii, however, the islanders stole one of his small boats. Cook planned to take the local king hostage to get his boat back. As Cook negotiated, his crew opened fire and the islanders stabbed Cook to death.

Knives are drawn as Cook's men open fire.

So close, yet so far!

Many people believed Australia was so vast it must contain an inland sea. In 1860, the South Australian government decided to find out. It offered a large cash prize to the first person to cross the continent from south to north.

Early setbacks

Robert Burke's expedition seemed well equipped. It set out from Melbourne with 18 men, 24 camels, 28 horses, and 21 tons of provisions. But when the camel master and the doctor quit at Menindee, 400 miles north of Melbourne, Burke left most of his supplies behind and continued with a small group. At Cooper's Creek, he left William Brahe in charge of the remaining party, and set out north with William Wills, John King, Charles Gray, and provisions for 12 weeks.

The mudflats at the Gulf of Carpentaria.

Time Line

August 21, 1860
Burke's expedition sets out from Melbourne

October 19, 1860
Two men drop out at Menindee

December 16, 1860
Burke establishes supply depot at Cooper's Creek

February 9, 1861
Expedition reaches the tidal Flinders River but does not see the sea

April 21, 1861
Burke, Wills, and King return to find Cooper's Creek deserted

June 1861
Burke and Wills die of starvation; King is rescued by Aborigines

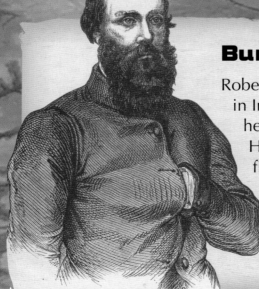

Burke and Wills

Robert O'Hara Burke (1821–61), left, was born in Ireland and emigrated to Australia, where he became a police officer in Melbourne. His expedition into the interior was his first experience of the Australian outback (remote dry areas). William John Wills (1834–61), right, became Burke's second in command when the camel master defected.

Beasts of burden

Camels are not native to Australia, but were introduced in the 1840s to carry goods in the outback. Some of them escaped—these were the ancestors of Australia's wild camel population.

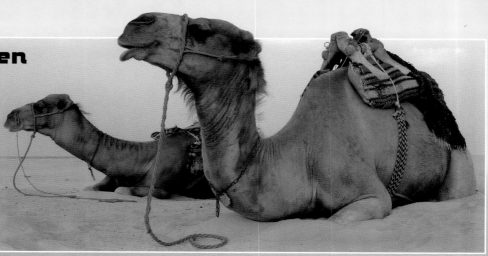

Almost there

On February 9, 1861, Burke's party reached the tidal estuary of the Flinders River in the Gulf of Carpentaria. They never saw the coast because wide mudflats stood between them and the sea. Almost immediately they headed south again, with Gray dying of dysentery on the way. In April, they arrived at Cooper's Creek to find it deserted. Within two months, Burke and Wills had both died of starvation.

DiscoveryFact™

Robert Burke was criticized for his poor handling of the expedition, but both he and Wills were later recognized for their bravery by a memorial in Melbourne.

Lost in the bush

When Burke and his two colleagues arrived back in Cooper's Creek, William Brahe had left just hours earlier. Wills and King wanted to try to catch up with him, but Burke insisted on heading for Mount Hopeless 150 miles to the southwest. Their food ran out, and Burke and Wills died. King was rescued when he was found by Aborigines.

Burke, Wills, and King were lost in the bush. Only King survived.

McDouall Stuart

Scottish-born John McDouall Stuart (1815–66) moved to South Australia in 1838 to work as a surveyor. In 1844, he joined Charles Sturt, who was an English explorer, on his unsuccessful expedition to reach the center of the continent.

The prize

The prize offered by the South Australian government to cross the continent from south to north proved irresistible to John Stuart. He was so determined to win, he made three attempts in just two years!

Failed expedition

In March 1860, Stuart set out from Adelaide in South Australia with just two travel companions. A month later, he made it just over halfway there, reaching Tenant Creek. Here, he had to turn back because Aborigines had set fire to the bush in front of him to defend their land.

The British flag is raised in triumph on the shores of the Indian Ocean.

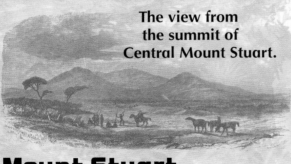

The view from the summit of Central Mount Stuart.

Mount Stuart

On his first attempt to cross Australia, Stuart reached the exact center of the continent. He named a nearby hill Central Mount Sturt "after the father of Australian exploration." The hill was later renamed Central Mount Stuart after its discoverer.

Pride of Adelaide

The city of Adelaide was founded in 1836, when the British established a colony in South Australia. The city was anxious to make its mark on Australian history, so it offered the prize to cross the continent in 1860.

A statue of John McDouall Stuart in Adelaide.

Try and try again

On his second attempt in early 1861, with a party of 13 men and 49 horses, Stuart came within 200 miles of the sea, but turned back when a thicket of thorn bushes blocked his way. In October 1861, he tried again. This time he reached the north coast of Australia at Chambers Bay. The continent had been successfully crossed at last.

Time Line

March 2, 1860
Stuart and two companions leave Adelaide to cross Australia, but turn back halfway

January 1, 1861
Stuart sets off again

September 1861
Returns to Adelaide 200 miles short of the north coast

October 1861
Begins third attempt to cross Australia

July 1862
Reaches Indian Ocean

December 1862
Returns home, having lost the use of his limbs due to scurvy

DiscoveryFact™

An overland telegraph line was opened along Stuart's route nine years later. From Darwin on the north coast, the line ran under the sea, connecting Australia to Indonesia and Asia.

Searching for the source

The source of the Nile River fascinated explorers in East Africa. Everyone knew about its route through Egypt to the Mediterranean Sea, but where did this great river start?

James Bruce

Scotsman James Bruce (1730–94) started traveling after his wife died. He visited Spain and Portugal. When his father died four years later, he inherited enough money to travel full time. He first visited Africa in 1763.

Into Abyssinia

James Bruce was one of the first explorers to search for the source of the Nile. In 1768, he set off with about 20 men from Cairo up the Nile to the first set of cataracts (waterfalls) on the river at Aswan. He then headed east across the desert to the Red Sea. There, he hired a ship to take him to Massawa, in what is now Eritrea. The party then headed inland to Gondar, capital of Abyssinia (now Ethiopia). Here, he was granted the protection of the ruling emperor and helped in the country's civil war.

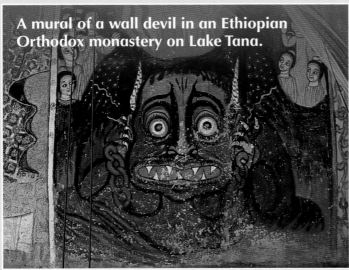

A mural of a wall devil in an Ethiopian Orthodox monastery on Lake Tana.

Land of monks

Lake Tana in northwest Ethiopia is fed by more than 60 streams, one of which is regarded as the source of the Blue Nile River. James Bruce recorded that there were as many as 45 inhabited islands on the lake, many with Christian monasteries on them.

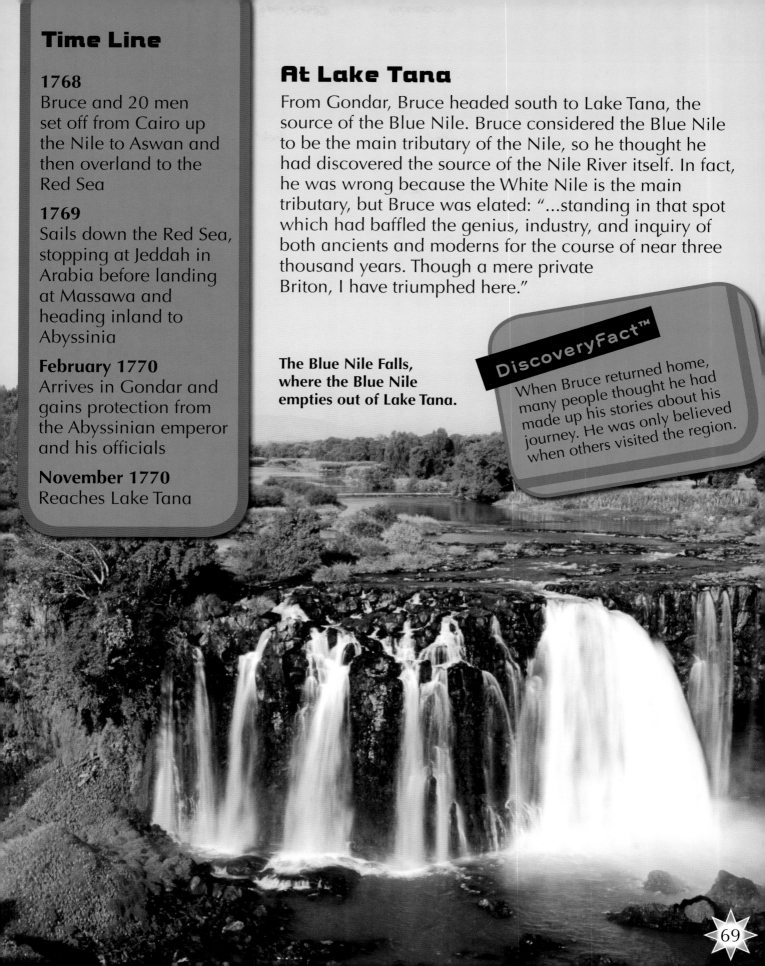

Time Line

1768
Bruce and 20 men set off from Cairo up the Nile to Aswan and then overland to the Red Sea

1769
Sails down the Red Sea, stopping at Jeddah in Arabia before landing at Massawa and heading inland to Abyssinia

February 1770
Arrives in Gondar and gains protection from the Abyssinian emperor and his officials

November 1770
Reaches Lake Tana

At Lake Tana

From Gondar, Bruce headed south to Lake Tana, the source of the Blue Nile. Bruce considered the Blue Nile to be the main tributary of the Nile, so he thought he had discovered the source of the Nile River itself. In fact, he was wrong because the White Nile is the main tributary, but Bruce was elated: "...standing in that spot which had baffled the genius, industry, and inquiry of both ancients and moderns for the course of near three thousand years. Though a mere private Briton, I have triumphed here."

The Blue Nile Falls, where the Blue Nile empties out of Lake Tana.

DiscoveryFact™

When Bruce returned home, many people thought he had made up his stories about his journey. He was only believed when others visited the region.

Mission accomplished

John Speke was sure he had found the source of the Nile in Lake Victoria in 1858. Some people back in London, however, wanted more proof so he returned to Africa to find it.

The true source of the Nile

Speke set off in 1860 accompanied by James Grant. They traveled around the western edge of Lake Victoria. Grant was forced to rest due to an infected leg, so he was not with Speke in July 1862 when he found a waterfall at the northern end of the lake. It led down to a river—this was the start of the Nile.

James Grant

James Grant (1827–92) met John Speke while serving in the British army in India. After Speke's death, Grant defended his friend's achievements until Henry Stanley proved Speke right in 1875.

Grant and Speke negotiate a safe passage with the Queen Dowager of Uganda.

Hippos are among the many animals that live in and by the White Nile.

The White Nile

The most distant stream of the White Nile (the major tributary of the Nile) starts in the Nyungwe Forest in southern Rwanda. It flows out of Lake Victoria and then north until it meets the Blue Nile at Khartoum. The river gets its name from the particles of whitish clay suspended in its waters.

Time Line

April 1860
Speke and Grant depart for East Africa

1861
Reach Kaweh and head north around western edge of Lake Victoria; Grant becomes ill

July 28, 1862
Speke discovers and names the Ripon Falls

February 1863
The two arrive in Gondokoro in Sudan, and meet Samuel and Florence Baker

March 1864
The Bakers discover the Murchison Falls and Lake Albert

September 15, 1864
Speke accidentally shoots himself

A tragic accident

Back in London, Speke and Grant were treated as heroes. But not everyone was convinced that they had found the source of the Nile. Their most prominent critic was Richard Burton, who insisted that they had not proved that the river emerged from Lake Victoria. The pair agreed to debate the issue in public. The day before the debate, however, Speke accidentally shot himself.

Filling in the gaps

The Royal Geographical Society asked Samuel and Florence Baker to search for Speke and Grant, who had not been heard of for a year. After finding them, the Bakers explored parts of the Nile that Speke had not visited. They found that the river flows from Lake Victoria, down through the Murchison Falls, before heading north into Sudan.

The Murchison Falls, where the water is channeled through a 23-foot-wide gap in the rocks.

Livingstone in Africa

David Livingstone was first and foremost a doctor and missionary, but he was also a superb explorer. The books he wrote about his four great journeys brought Africa to European attention. His fight against the Arab-run slave trade eventually ended that cruel practice.

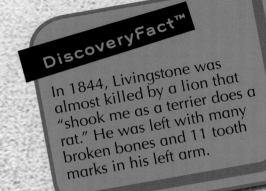

DiscoveryFact™

In 1844, Livingstone was almost killed by a lion that "shook me as a terrier does a rat." He was left with many broken bones and 11 tooth marks in his left arm.

Time Line

March 14, 1841
Livingstone lands in Cape Town

1841–44
Explores Kalahari Desert

June 1849
Discovers Lake Ngami

April 1851
Discovers Zambezi River

November 1853
Sets off west from the Zambezi

May 31, 1854
Reaches Luanda in Angola, then heads east

May 20, 1856
Reaches Quelimane on Indian Ocean

August 1859
Discovers Lake Nyasa on third expedition

First journey

Livingstone arrived in Cape Town in 1841. He headed inland to work at a Christian mission at Kuruman at the edge of the Kalahari Desert. Three years later, he moved farther north to set up his own mission. He took every opportunity to explore the area. He became the first European to see Lake Ngami in northern Botswana and, in 1851, the Zambezi—a previously unknown river. At this point, he accompanied his wife and four children back to Cape Town to send them back to England.

David Livingstone

Dr. David Livingstone (1813–73) was born into a poor family in Blantyre, Scotland. At the age of 10, he was working 14 hours a day in a local cotton mill. He later worked part time in the mill while studying in Glasgow to be a doctor, so that he could become a medical missionary.

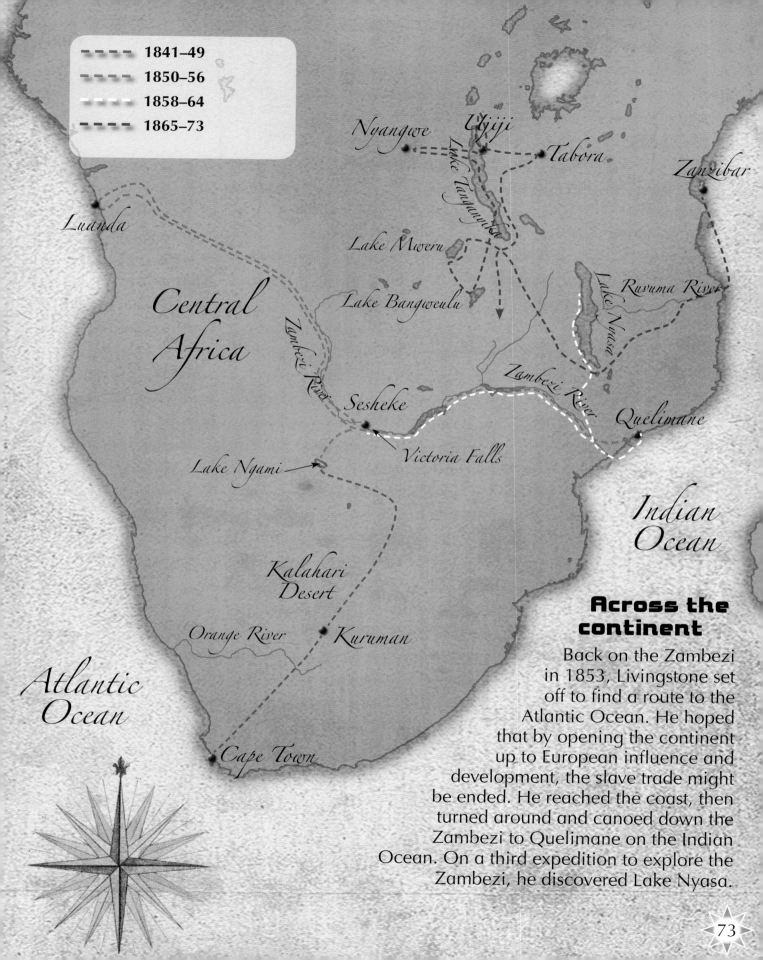

1841–49
1850–56
1858–64
1865–73

Nyangwe
Ujiji
Tabora
Zanzibar
Lake Tanganyika
Luanda
Lake Mweru
Ruvuma River
Central
Africa
Lake Bangweulu
Lake Nyasa
Zambezi River
Sesheke
Zambezi River
Quelimane
Victoria Falls
Lake Ngami
Indian
Ocean
Kalahari
Desert
Orange River
Kuruman

Atlantic
Ocean

Across the continent

Back on the Zambezi in 1853, Livingstone set off to find a route to the Atlantic Ocean. He hoped that by opening the continent up to European influence and development, the slave trade might be ended. He reached the coast, then turned around and canoed down the Zambezi to Quelimane on the Indian Ocean. On a third expedition to explore the Zambezi, he discovered Lake Nyasa.

Cape Town

Dr. Livingstone?

In 1865, David Livingstone set out on his fourth and final journey. This time his aim was to find the source of three great African rivers: the Congo, Zambezi, and Nile. John Speke had discovered the Nile's source, but many still doubted him. Livingstone set off to find out for himself.

A futile search

Livingstone started his journey on the Ruvuma River—the boundary between Tanzania and Mozambique—before trekking north to Lake Tanganyika. He spent the next three years exploring this and other lakes in the region and trying to work out which one was the source of the Nile. In fact, none was because most of them drained into the Congo.

Livingstone became so ill that he often had to be carried on a stretcher by his companions.

The final journey

By the end of his life, Livingstone was weak with fever and becoming increasingly confused. For the first time ever, he got lost when his chronometers were accidentally damaged, and his sextant developed a fault. But he was still driven to travel in his quest to end the slave trade.

A 19th-century painting based on Livingstone's description of the moment he and Stanley first met.

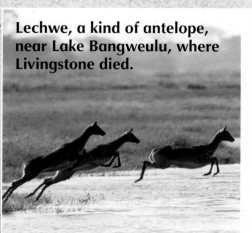

Lechwe, a kind of antelope, near Lake Bangweulu, where Livingstone died.

Livingstone's end

When Livingstone died, his companions Chuma and Susi carried his body 600 miles to the coast so that it could be taken to Great Britain. As he had requested, his heart was buried under a tree in a village near Lake Bangweulu.

A famous meeting

Livingstone had been out of touch with the rest of the world since 1869, so in 1871 an American newspaper hired Henry Stanley to seek him out. The pair met on November 10, 1871, at Ujiji. Stanley later reported that he was so overwhelmed, he took off his hat and uttered the famous words: "Dr. Livingstone, I presume?"

Time Line

March 22, 1866
Livingstone lands on East African coast

August 8, 1866
Reaches Lake Nyasa

April 1, 1867
Livingstone reaches Lake Tanganyika

November 1867
Reaches Lake Mweru

July 18, 1868
First sees Lake Bangweulu

March 29, 1871
Arrives in Nyangwe, the most northerly point in his travels

November 10, 1871
Meets Stanley at Ujiji

May 1, 1873
Livingstone dies near Lake Bangweulu

Livingstone's legacy

Although Livingstone did not discover the source of any major river, end the slave trade, or establish permanent missions, he did add a vast amount to European knowledge of Africa. He discovered several lakes and charted the Zambezi and other rivers. Soon after his death, the slave trade dramatically declined.

A statue of Livingstone at Victoria Falls.

DiscoveryFact™

A month after Livingstone's death, the British closed down the slave market in Zanzibar, the busiest in Africa.

Quick Quiz

Are these sentences TRUE or FALSE?
Place the correct sticker in the box.

1. There are only 80 giant statues on Easter Island.
2. Captain Cook's crew saw kangaroos on their travels.
3. Captain Cook had some islands named after him.
4. Camels are native to Australia.
5. James Bruce wanted to find the source of the Nile.

Match the stickers to these famous explorers and rulers.

Abel Tasman

Captain James Cook

Robert O'Hara Burke

McDouall Stuart

James Bruce

ANSWERS: 1−F, 2−T, 3−T, 4−F, 5−T

Extreme exploration

By the start of the 20th century, most of the world's land had been explored and mapped. However, the polar regions remained unconquered. Explorers also found new challenges by diving in the oceans and descending to their greatest depths, and climbing the highest mountains. With the arrival of space travel, we have been able to explore our moon and, using unmanned craft, our solar system and the stars beyond it.

Reaching the Pole

The race for the North Pole carried on into the early years of the 20th century. It was eventually won by the American explorer Robert Peary in 1909. Controversy continues to rage around his achievement, however, with some historians doubting that he ever reached the Pole at all.

Robert Peary

Robert Peary (1836–1920) devoted himself to Arctic exploration for a quarter of a century. He had trained as a civil engineer and worked for the navy before beginning his Arctic quest. He paid for his expeditions by writing about his adventures in books and magazines.

Preparing for the Pole

In a series of expeditions starting in 1886, Robert Peary pushed farther north. Each time he learned more about how to survive in the Arctic. By 1909, he was ready for the final attempt. The clothes, sleeping quarters, food, dogs, and sleds were=-- chosen specially for this expedition. The 24-man team left base camp on Ellesmere Island in March 1909, and set up a series of supply camps along two-thirds of the route to the Pole.

Matthew Henson

Matthew Henson (1866–1955) was an African American born into poverty. At first, Henson worked for Peary as a valet but he soon took responsibility for organizing his expeditions.

Racing there and back

The expedition traveled quickly over the hard ice, allowing Peary, Henson, and four local Inuit to make the final 155 miles to the Pole. After five days, on April 6, 1909, they set up camp 3 miles from the Pole. They crossed the Pole the next day before heading back to Cape Columbia, covering 70 miles in one day. Some doubt that Peary could travel at such a speed.

This drawing was made from a photograph taken by Peary of the four Inuit in the team that reached the Pole.

Time Line

April 1908
Peary and his expedition drop anchor near Cape Sheridan on Ellesmere Island; they then build a base camp farther north at Cape Columbia

March 1, 1909
The expedition leaves base camp

April 2
Peary, Henson, and four Inuit make the final dash to the Pole

April 6
Establish camp just short of the Pole

April 7
Peary stays in the area for 30 hours to make the calculations to prove he is at the Pole

April 23
Peary and team return to base camp

DiscoveryFact™

If Peary did not really reach the Pole, the first man who did was the British explorer Wally Herbert in 1969.

Race to the Pole

With the North Pole reached in 1909, only the South Pole remained unconquered. Its harsh, unforgiving climate had already defeated several expeditions, but in 1910 two well-equipped teams set out for the Pole. It was to be a race to the death.

The race begins

The first team was led by Roald Amundsen, the Norwegian hero of the Northwest Passage. Leaving the Bay of Whales on the east side of the Ross Sea on October 19, 1911, he headed across the ice shelf and up to the polar plateau. Just under two weeks later, a British expedition led by Robert Scott set out from the western end of the Ross Sea in McMurdo Sound and made their way onto the plateau.

Robert Scott

Captain Scott (1868–1912) was already an experienced Antarctic explorer by the time he set off for the Pole in 1911. He had taken part in a major expedition with Ernest Shackleton in 1901–4.

A heavy load

Robert Scott's expedition was not as well prepared as Amundsen's and relied mainly on Siberian ponies to pull their supplies. The ponies soon died of cold, forcing his team to pull the supplies on skis. Amundsen used skills learned from the Inuit in the Arctic and took huskies instead.

Scott's party pull their heavy sleds across the ice.

Amundsen originally intended to conquer the North Pole using Nansen's unique ship the *Fram*. When he heard that Peary had beaten him to it, he changed his plan and headed south instead.

Time Line

October 19, 1911
Amundsen's team sets off from Bay of Whales

November 1, 1911
Scott's team leave their base by McMurdo Sound

December 14, 1911
Amundsen and team reach the South Pole

January 11, 1912
Amundsen returns to base camp

January 17, 1912
Scott reaches the Pole

March 17, 1912
The sick Captain Oates walks out of the camp to die in the snow

March 29, 1912
Scott and two remaining companions die

SOUTH POLE

Scott's last supply depot
January 14, 1912

Amundsen's last supply depot
December 8, 1911

Polar Plateau

Transantarctic Mountains

A N T A R C T I C A

Ross Ice Shelf

Scott's last camp
March 19, 1912

Bay of Whales

ROSS SEA

McMurdo Sound

A Norwegian triumph

Amundsen's better preparations gave him the edge over Scott. His team arrived first at the Pole on December 14, 1911. They were back at their base camp by the time Scott reached the Pole on January 17, 1912. Tired and despondent, Scott and his team all died on the return journey, the last three within only 11 miles of safety.

Amundsen's team

Scott's team

To the bottom of the oceans

It is difficult for divers to operate deep under the sea, because the pressure on a diver's lungs is intense and the water is cold and dark. As a result, the deep seas remained almost entirely unknown until a new invention made underwater exploration possible in the 1930s.

Time Line

June 6, 1930
The bathysphere makes its first deep-sea dive off Nonsuch Island in Bermuda

1934
Barton and Beebe make a world's record descent of 3,028 feet off Bermuda, a record for 15 years

1953
The bathyscaphe *Trieste* is launched in Italy

January 23, 1960
With Auguste Piccard's son Jacques and Don Walsh of the U.S. Navy on board, the *Trieste* reaches the ocean floor of the Challenger Deep —the deepest part of the Mariana Trench

The bathysphere

The bathysphere was developed in 1930 by two Americans—the scientist William Beebe and the diver Otis Barton. It consisted of a metal sphere lowered into the water on a steel cable attached to a surface ship. Once they are sealed inside, the divers breathe oxygen from a high-pressure cylinder. They made their first descent in the waters off Bermuda in 1930.

William Beebe (left) and Otis Barton next to the bathysphere.

William Beebe

William Beebe (1877–1962) was curator of ornithology at the New York Zoological Society, but he was interested in far more than just birds. He made 35 dives in the bathysphere to observe the marine life of the Atlantic Ocean.

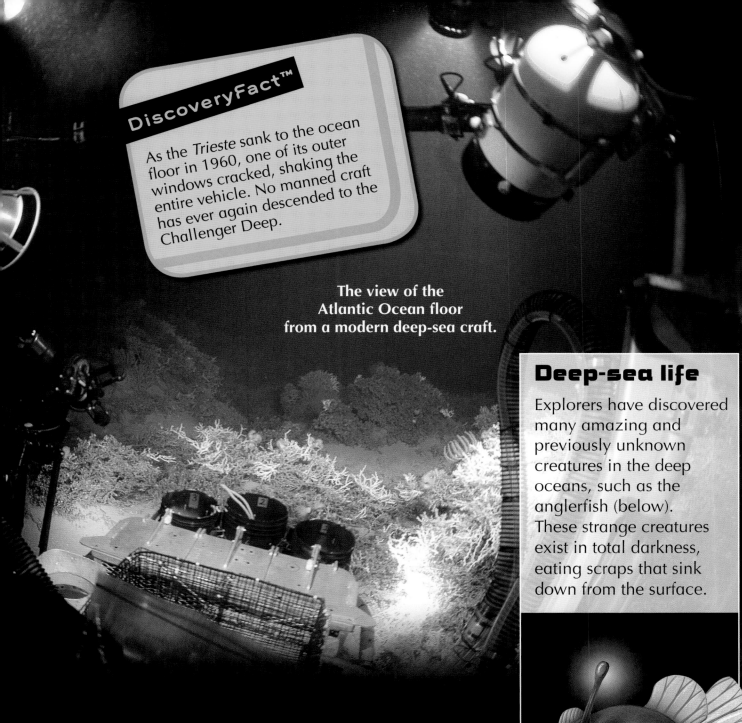

As the *Trieste* sank to the ocean floor in 1960, one of its outer windows cracked, shaking the entire vehicle. No manned craft has ever again descended to the Challenger Deep.

The view of the Atlantic Ocean floor from a modern deep-sea craft.

Deep-sea life

Explorers have discovered many amazing and previously unknown creatures in the deep oceans, such as the anglerfish (below). These strange creatures exist in total darkness, eating scraps that sink down from the surface.

The bathyscaphe

In 1953, Swiss scientist Auguste Piccard (1884–1962) developed the bathyscaphe. This craft used floodable tanks to move independently in the deepest of waters. In 1960, the *Trieste* bathyscaphe reached the deepest part of the world's oceans, the Challenger Deep in the Pacific Ocean, 35,797 feet (10,911 m) below sea level.

The top of the world

The high mountains of the Himalayas in Asia have long fascinated European explorers. Different nations concentrated on different Himalayan peaks: the Germans on Nanga Parbat, the Italians on K2—the second highest mountain in the world—and the British on Everest—the highest of them all.

Preparing the way

In the years after the end of World War I in 1918, 13 expeditions attempted—and failed—to reach the summit of Everest, all from the Tibetan side. In 1949, Nepal opened up its borders to Europeans, allowing climbers to tackle Everest from its side of the border. The following year, French climbers reached the top of Annapurna I, breaking the psychological 26,250 feet barrier. The way was now clear to tackle Everest.

Time Line

March 10, 1953
Expedition led by John Hunt leaves Katmandu and treks through the Himalayan foothills

March 25
Expedition sets up base camp on the Khunbu glacier at 18,145 feet

May 28
Hillary and Tenzing set off; support team stops at 28,051 feet

May 29
Hillary and Tenzing reach the summit at 11:30 a.m. and spend 15 minutes there before descending

Tenzing and Hillary

Tenzing Norgay (1914–86), left, was a Nepalese with a vast experience of Himalayan climbing. He reached to within 820 feet of the summit with a Swiss expedition in 1952. Edmund Hillary (1919–2008), right, was born in Auckland, New Zealand, and climbed his first major mountain at the age of 20. In 1950, he climbed in the Alps and made his first visit to the Himalayas in 1951.

Reaching the summit

The expedition in 1953 was carefully planned, with a series of supply camps established up to the South Crest at 28,051 feet. From there, two climbers would climb the final 984 feet to the summit. Accompanied by a support group, Edmund Hillary and Tenzing Norgay set out on May 28, spending that night on a narrow, snow-covered ledge. The next morning was clear as the pair climbed to the summit.

A supply camp on a modern expedition to climb Everest.

Mount Everest, at 29,035 feet is the highest mountain in the world.

DiscoveryFact™

Since the conquest of Everest in 1953, the mountain has been climbed almost every year. On May 15, 2002, 54 climbers reached the summit on the same day.

Supply camps

The 1953 expedition established a series of nine camps between base camp at the foot of the Khunbu glacier and the summit. Each camp was supplied with food and equipment necessary for the climb, including oxygen tanks for the climbers.

Mountain guides

Tenzing Norgay was a Sherpa. The Sherpa are an ethnic group from the Himalayan region of Nepal. Their ancestors migrated to Nepal from eastern Tibet about 500 years ago. The Sherpa are tough, hardy people very used to the high altitudes of the Himalayas, and they are valuable guides and porters on mountaineering expeditions in the region.

The Sherpa are used to making long journeys on foot at high altitudes.

Into space

The attention of many potential explorers turned toward the heavens and into space after 1945. The technological advances required to send a man into orbit around the world, let alone to the Moon, and then bring him safely back to Earth were immense.

The Space Race

Near the end of the World War II, Germany had developed the technology to fire V-2 rockets at supersonic speeds within Earth's atmosphere. Once the war ended, scientists used this technology to build rockets capable of escaping Earth's gravity and traveling through space. A competition began between the United States and Russia (then known as the USSR) to put a man into space.

Time Line

October 4, 1957
USSR launches the world's first artificial satellite, *Sputnik I*

November 1957
A dog named Laika is the first living creature in space on *Sputnik II*, but dies in orbit

August 20, 1960
Sputnik V carries two dogs into orbit, and brings them back to Earth safely

April 12, 1961
Yuri Gagarin becomes the first person in space, orbiting the Earth once on board *Vostok I*

Yuri Gagarin

Yuri Gagarin (1934–68) was born in western Russia and qualified as a military pilot in 1957. He was chosen along with 19 other cosmonauts in 1960 to join the Soviet space program. His successful space flight in 1961 made him into an international celebrity. He died on a military training flight seven years later.

Two firsts

The USSR launched the world's first artificial satellite (object that orbits Earth), *Sputnik I*, in 1957. Four years later, cosmonaut Yuri Gagarin was the first man to be sent into space on board a *Vostok* spaceship. The United States sent its first astronaut, Alan Shepard, into space a few months after Gagarin, but the USSR had established a clear lead in the Space Race.

Earth seen from space.

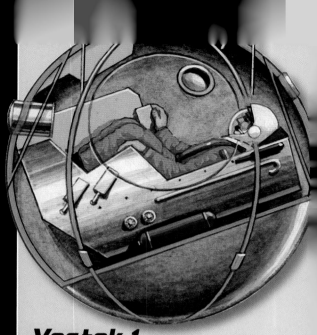

Vostok 1

The spherical *Vostok* spacecraft that took Yuri Gagarin into space was launched from the Baikonur Cosmodrome. The flight lasted 108 minutes. It ended when Gagarin ejected from the capsule. He was 4 miles above the ground and had to parachute to safety.

DiscoveryFact™

The first two living creatures to survive going into space and reentering Earth's atmosphere were the dogs Belka and Strelka in 1960.

Sputnik 1

Sputnik I was launched on top of a rocket from the Baikonur Cosmodrome in what is now Kazakhstan on October 4, 1957. The spherical satellite only measured 23 inches in diameter. It traveled at 18,000 mph and broadcast radio signals for 22 days until its transmitter batteries ran out.

A man on the Moon

In May 1961, President John F. Kennedy committed the United States to landing a man on the Moon by the end of the decade. The Americans were behind the USSR in the space race, so the Apollo space program was devised to help them to catch up.

The Apollo program

The Apollo space program was the most ambitious project that any nation had undertaken in peacetime. At its peak, almost half a million people worked for it. Their goal was to design a craft that would carry three human beings to the Moon, 236,100 miles away.

Apollo 11 **was launched on the 365-foot-tall, three-stage Saturn V rocket.**

Tragic beginnings

The first launch in 1967 was a disaster. The three astronauts were killed when a fire broke out on the launchpad. Subsequent flights put astronauts into orbit around the Earth, then the Moon, testing the equipment they would need to land on the Moon.

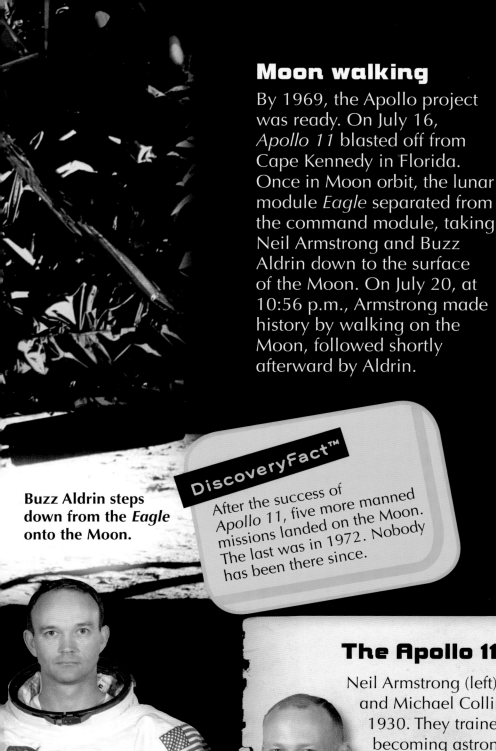

Moon walking

By 1969, the Apollo project was ready. On July 16, *Apollo 11* blasted off from Cape Kennedy in Florida. Once in Moon orbit, the lunar module *Eagle* separated from the command module, taking Neil Armstrong and Buzz Aldrin down to the surface of the Moon. On July 20, at 10:56 p.m., Armstrong made history by walking on the Moon, followed shortly afterward by Aldrin.

Buzz Aldrin steps down from the *Eagle* onto the Moon.

DiscoveryFact™

After the success of *Apollo 11*, five more manned missions landed on the Moon. The last was in 1972. Nobody has been there since.

Time Line

January 27, 1967
Apollo 1 catches fire on the launchpad, killing the three astronauts on board

October 11, 1968
Apollo 7 makes manned flight around Earth

December 21, 1968
Apollo 8 makes first manned flight around the Moon

July 20, 1969
Apollo 11 makes first Moon landing

July 26, 1971
Apollo 15 sends a rover vehicle to explore the surface of the Moon

December 7, 1972
Apollo 17 makes final Apollo mission

The Apollo 11 crew

Neil Armstrong (left), Edwin "Buzz" Aldrin (right), and Michael Collins (center), were all born in 1930. They trained as military pilots before becoming astronauts, making their first space flights in the Gemini program in 1966. While the other two astronauts descended to the Moon on board the lunar module *Eagle*, Collins remained in orbit around the Moon on board the Columbia command module.

Quick Quiz

Are these sentences TRUE or FALSE?
Place the correct sticker in the box.

1. ☐ Robert Peary traveled to the South Pole.
2. ☐ The South Pole was reached in 1911.
3. ☐ The bathysphere was invented for deep sea exploration.
4. ☐ Mount Everest is the third highest mountain in the world.
5. ☐ Yuri Gagarin was the first person to orbit space.

Match the stickers to these famous explorers.

Matthew Henson

Robert Scott

William Bebe

Tenzing Norgay

Neil Armstrong

Glossary

Archipelago
Large group of islands.

Arctic Circle
Imaginary line around the North Pole that marks the limit of the region that experiences 24-hour darkness in midwinter.

c.
Abbreviation for the Latin word circa, meaning about. It is used when an exact date is unknown.

Chronometer
Watch designed to be accurate in all climate conditions.

Circumnavigation
Journey made around the world.

Colony
Region or country that is controlled by another country.

Continent
One of the seven great landmasses of the world: North America, South America, Europe, Africa, Asia, Australasia (Oceania), and Antarctica.

Czar
The hereditary emperor or ruler of Russia. Also spelled tsar.

Empire
Many different lands and countries ruled over by one leader.

Equator
Imaginary line around Earth at an equal distance between the North and South Poles.

Galleon
Large sailing ship used as a warship or merchant ship.

Headwaters
Streams that flow into one another to start a river.

Hydrography
The study of Earth's oceans, seas, and rivers.

Isthmus
Narrow strip of land connecting two larger areas of land.

Knot
A speed of one nautical mile per hour. A nautical mile is equal to 6,076 feet

Latitude
The distance north or south of the equator, measured in degrees.

Log
Detailed record of a ship's voyage, updated daily or sometimes hourly.

Longitude
The distance east or west of an imaginary line that runs from the North to the South Pole through Greenwich in England.

Magnetic South Pole
Place to which all compasses in the southern hemisphere point.

Missionary
A person who travels to convert the local people to his or her religion.

New World
Term used by Europeans to describe North America after they first visited it in the 16th century.

Northern hemisphere
The half of Earth that lies north of the equator.

North Pole
The northernmost point of Earth's axis of rotation, which lies in the center of Arctic Circle.

Oceanography
Study of the world's oceans.

Pack ice
Ice floating in huge sheets, found in the Arctic and Antarctic.

Peninsula
Narrow strip of land surrounded by water on three sides.

Pilgrimage
Journey to a shrine or other sacred place, made by a pilgrim.

Polar
Relating to the North or South Poles.

Quadrant
Navigation instrument used by sailors to calculate the angle of a star so that they can work out a ship's latitude. The quadrant was replaced in the 18th century by the octant, and then the more accurate sextant.

Schooner
Sailing vessel with at least two masts. All the lower sails on a schooner are rigged from front to back.

Scurvy
Disease caused by a lack of vitamin C, which often used to affect sailors when they did not eat fresh fruit or vegetables.

Scuttle
To deliberately sink a ship to stop it from falling into enemy hands.

Silk Road
Ancient trade route linking China through central Asia and the Middle East to the Mediterranean and on to Europe.

Sloop
A single-masted sailing vessel.

Source
The spring or headwaters from which a river begins.

Southern hemisphere
The half of Earth that lies south of the equator.

South Pole
Southernmost point of Earth's axis of rotation, which lies in Antarctica.

Square-rigged
Ship rigged with square or rectangular sails, often hanging from a solid beam.

Strait
Narrow channel of water between two seas or oceans.

Treasure ship
Galleon or other large ship used to carry gold, silver, and other precious goods.

Trimaran
Yacht with three hulls, usually with a main hull flanked by two smaller hulls.

Timeline

c. **1470 B.C.**	Egyptians sail to Punt
c. **475 B.C.**	Hanno sails down west coast of Africa
c. **330 B.C.**	Pytheas sails around Britain; visits Thule
c. **200 B.C.**	Polynesians settle Tahiti
138 B.C.	Zhang Qian travels through central Asia
A.D. 399	Faxian travels from China to India
A.D. 629	Xuanzang travels from China to India
A.D. 921	Ibn Fadlan travels through central Asia
*c.***1000**	Leif Erikson sails to Vinland
1253	William of Rubruck visits the Great Khan
1271	Marco Polo sets out for China
1325	Ibn Battuta sets off from Tangier for Mecca

1405	Zheng He starts the first of his seven voyages
1418	Henry the Navigator founds school at Sagres
1486	Diogo Cão sails to Cape Cross in Namibia
1488	Bartolomeu Dias rounds Cape of Good Hope
1492	Christopher Columbus sails across Atlantic
1497	Vasco da Gama opens up sea route to India; John Cabot sails to Newfoundland
1499	Amerigo Vespucci sails along coast of Brazil
1513	Núñez de Balboa sights the Pacific Ocean
1519	Ferdinand Magellan sets out west from Europe
1521	Hernán Cortés seizes Aztec Empire
1522	Delcano completes first circumnavigation

1785	Comte de La Pérouse explores the Pacific
1796	Mungo Park reaches the Niger
1804	Lewis and Clark cross North America
1812	Johann Ludwig Burckhardt visits Petra
1828	Charles Sturt begins to map Australian rivers; René Caillié enters Timbuktu
1830	Richard Lander follows the Niger to the sea
1835	Charles Darwin visits the Galápagos Islands
1838	Charles Wilkes leads scientific expedition
1841	Edward Eyre crosses Australia east–west; David Livingstone begins to explore Africa
1842	John Frémont starts to open up western United States

1850	Heinrich Barth sets out across the Sahara
1858	Richard Burton first sees Lake Tanganyika
1860	Burke and Wills cross Australia south–north
1861	John Stuart raises British flag near Darwin
1862	John Speke discovers the source of the Nile
1871	Livingstone and Henry Stanley meet at Ujiji; Charles Hall reaches north shore of Greenland
1872	HMS Challenger explores the world's oceans
1876	Henry Stanley starts to explore the Congo
1879	Adolf Nordenskiöld sails Northeast Passage
1890	Sven Hedin sets out for central Asia
1893	Fridtjof Nansen begins journey on the Fram; Mary Kingsley first sets out for West Africa

1528	Pánfilo de Narváez explores Florida	1642	Abel Tasman sails around Australia
1533	Francisco Pizarro seizes Inca Empire	1661	Grueber and D'Orville visit Lhasa
1535	Jacques Cartier searches for Northwest Passage	1673	Louis Jolliet explores the Mississippi
1541	Francis Xavier travels through Asia	1674	William Dampier begins circumnavigation
1553	Richard Chancellor finds sea route to Russia	1682	Cavelier de La Salle reaches the Mississippi Delta
1554	Alvaro de Mendaña sails across the Pacific	1725	Vitus Bering journeys to Siberia
1577	Francis Drake begins circumnavigation	1740	George Anson sets sail around the world
1594	Willem Barents searches for Northeast Passage	1766	John Byron completes circumnavigation; Louis-Antoine de Bougainville sets out to colonize South Pacific from France
1603	Samuel de Champlain explores Canada		
1607	Luis Váez de Torres sails around New Guinea	1768	James Cook sets sail for the Pacific
1610	Henry Hudson discovers the Hudson Strait	1770	James Bruce discovers the source of the Blue Nile
1624	Antonio de Andrade crosses the Himalayas		

1895	Joshua Slocum sets out on solo voyage around the world	1947	Thor Heyerdahl crosses Pacific on Kon-Tiki
1899	Gertrude Bell starts to explore Middle East	1953	Hillary and Tenzing climb Everest
1900	Aurel Stein starts to explore western China	1957	USSR launches first satellite, Sputnik 1
1906	Roald Amundsen navigates Northwest Passage	1958	Vivian Fuchs crosses Antarctica
1909	Peary and Henson reach North Pole	1960	Trieste descends to bottom of Mariana Trench
1911	Roald Amundsen reaches South Pole	1961	Yuri Gagarin is first man in space
1927	Freya Stark travels through Arabian desert	1967	Francis Chichester completes first solo, one-stop circumnavigation
1930	Bertram Thomas crosses Empty Quarter; Beebe and Barton make their first descent in the bathysphere in the waters off Bermuda	1969	Robin Knox-Johnston completes first solo, nonstop circumnavigation; Armstrong and Aldrin walk on the Moon
1943	Jacques Cousteau invents the aqualung	2008	Francis Joyon sets new solo record of 57 days for solo, nonstop circumnavigation
1945	Wilfred Thesiger explores the Empty Quarter		

Index

Acknowledgments

Artwork supplied by Martin McKenna, Michael Welply, and Mike White, and through Linden Artists by Adam Hook, Francis Phillipps, and Clive Spong.

Photo credits:
b = bottom, t = top, r = right, l = left, c = center

Cover images:
bl Standard RM/CORBIS, bc John Farmar/Cordaiy photo library/CORBIS, br Peter Hazlett/Dreamstime

Poster: guenterguni/istockphoto
1 Shilo Long/Dreamstime.com, 2-3 Alexander Potapov/Dreamstime.com, 6tr Pilar Echeverria/Dreamstime.com, 6b Bryan Busovicki/istockphoto, 6-7 Martin Brown/Dreamstime.com 7t NASA, 7cr NASA, 7b Burillier 7br Robb Cox/istockphoto.com, 6–7 Keren Su/CORBIS, 8–9 Vladimir Korostyshevskiy/Dreamstime.com,8t Andrew Kershaw/Dreamstime.com, 8b Michał Kram/Dreamstime.com, 10–11 BishkekRocks, 10b Bettmann/CORBIS, 13 Werner Forman/CORBIS,14t Denise Kappa/istockphoto, 15t Erik Torpegaard, 15b Dylan Kereluk/creativecommons.org, 16–17 Kazuyoshi Nomachi/Corbis, 16b Pavel Bortel/Dreamstime.com, 17t Stefanie Van Der Vinden/Dreamstime.com, 19t Hulton-Deutsch Collection/ CORBIS, 20–21 Robert Churchill/iStockphoto, 21t Christopher Elwell/Dreamstime.com, 23 Krause, Johansen/Archivo Iconografico, SA/Corbis, 24–25 Archivo Iconografico, S.A./CORBIS, 24t Corbis,25t The Art Archive/Corbis, 26 Celso Pupo Rodrigues/Dreamstime.com, 27 Krause, Johansen/Archivo Iconografico, SA/Corbis, 28–29 John Van Hasselt/CORBIS SYGMA, 28b Bettmann/CORBIS, 29t Norbert Speicher/istockphoto, 30l Bettmann/CORBIS, 31t Tradkelly/Dreamstime.com, 34–35 Christopher Howey/Dreamstime.com, 34t Bettmann/CORBIS, 34b David Hughes/Dreamstime.com,35t John Farmar; Cordaiy Photo Library Ltd./CORBIS, 36–37 Stapleton Collection/Corbis, 36b NASA, 38–39 Historical Picture Archive/CORBIS, 39 Rodrigo roy a Boncato/Dreamstime.com, 41 Frans Lemmens/zefa/Corbis, 42–43 Charles & Josette Lenars/CORBIS, 43 The Art Archive/Corbis, 44–45 Bryan Busovicki/istockphoto, 44t Bettmann/CORBIS, 44b Carlos Santa Maria | Agency: Dreamstime.com, 45 Håkan Svensson, 46–47 Douglas Allen/istockphoto, 47b Burstein Collection/ CORBIS, 48t Bettmann/CORBIS, 48b Bettmann/CORBIS, 49t CORBIS, 49b NASA, 50–51 Martin Brown/dreamstime.com, 50b Independence National Historical Park, 51t Smithsonian American Art Museum, 51b Michael Thompson/Dreamstime.com, 53 Vladimir Kindrachov/Dreamstime.com, 54b Paul Chinn/San Francisco Chronicle/Corbis, 55t Jose Tejo/Dreamstime.com, 57b The Gallery Collection/Corbis, 58–59 Michael Willis/ istockphoto, 58l National Archive of Canada, 59t Adam Booth/istockphoto.com, 59b Natural History Museum London, 60–61 Alexander Putaya/Dreamstime.com, 60 Museum of History and Industry/CORBIS, 61t Stapleton Collection/Corbis, 62–63 Jeanne Hatch/istockphoto.com, 62l Oksanaphoto/Dreamstime.com, 63t Martyn Unsworth/istockphoto.com, 64–65 Chris Hellier/CORBIS, 65t Antonela Magzan/Dreamstime.com, 66t John McDouall Stuart Society, 67t John McDouall Stuart Society, 68–69 Torleif Svensson/CORBIS, 68t Krause, Johansen/Archivo Iconografico, SA/Corbis, 68b Jacob Eliosoff, 70t Stapleton Collection/Corbis, 71t Klaas Lingbeek-van Kranen/istockphoto.com, 71b Liz Leyden/ istockphoto, 72b Hulton archive/istockphoto.com, 74–75 Bettmann/CORBIS, 74b Nik Wheeler/CORBIS, 77 Bernard Breton/Dreamstime.com, 78–79 Stapleton Collection/Corbis, 78t US Library of Congress, 79t US Library of Congress, 80t Hulton-Deutsch Collection/CORBIS, 80b Bettmann/Corbis, 82–83 Dr. Steve Ross/NOAA, 82b Ralph White/CORBIS, 84–85 Jose Fuente/Dreamstime.com, 84b Bettmann/CORBIS, 85t Peter Hazlett/Dreamstime.com, 85b Robert Churchill/ istockphoto, 86–87 NASA, 88l NASA, 88–89t NASA, 88–89b NASA.